What in the World Happened in the Kingdom of Judah?

The Life and Times of Isaiah the Prophet

Virginia L. Smith, PhD
with
Jessica Karlyn Dill

TEACH Services, Inc.
P U B L I S H I N G
www.TEACHServices.com • (800) 367-1844

World rights reserved. This book or any portion thereof may not be copied or reproduced in any form or manner whatever, except as provided by law, without the written permission of the publisher, except by a reviewer who may quote brief passages in a review.

The author assumes full responsibility for the accuracy of all facts and quotations as cited in this book. The opinions expressed in this book are the author's personal views and interpretations, and do not necessarily reflect those of the publisher.

This book is provided with the understanding that the publisher is not engaged in giving spiritual, legal, medical, or other professional advice. If authoritative advice is needed, the reader should seek the counsel of a competent professional.

Copyright © 2023 Virginia L. Smith
Copyright © 2023 TEACH Services, Inc.
ISBN- 978-1-4796-1425-7 (Paperback)
ISBN- 978-1-4796-1426-4 (ePub)
Library of Congress Control Number: 2022919922

All Scripture quotations, unless otherwise noted, are taken from the NEW INTERNATIONAL VERSION (NIV): Scripture taken from THE HOLY BIBLE, NEW INTERNATIONAL VERSION®. Copyright ©1973, 1978, 1984, 2011 by Biblica, Inc.™ Used by permission of Zondervan Bible Publishers.

Scriptures marked ESV are taken from THE HOLY BIBLE, ENGLISH STANDARD VERSION (ESV): Scriptures taken from THE HOLY BIBLE, ENGLISH STANDARD VERSION® Copyright© Crossway, a publishing ministry of Good News Publishers. Used by permission.

Dedication

This book is dedicated to my mother, Ruth E. Schuler. She taught me to read at an early age, then always forgave me for reading when I was supposed to be doing something else. Furthermore, she brought home boxes of books at a time and kept me from going to the library to be exposed to other books that would not have advanced my education in the ways she saw fit. When she decided I needed to contribute something to the housekeeping, she always sent me to dust a bookcase. It could take me hours because I would soon be lost in one of the books.

Contents

Acknowledgements 7
Introduction 9
PART I: Uzziah and the Time of Prosperity 13
    Chapter One: Prologue. 14
    Chapter Two: Isaiah, the Young Man 22
PART II: Jotham, the King 41
    Chapter Three: Isaiah, the Prophet. 42
    Chapter Four: Isaiah Sees God 51
PART III: Ahaz, the King. 57
    Chapter Five: The Gloom of Night Approaches 58
    Chapter Six: The Depths of Night. 73
PART IV: Hezekiah, the King. 85
    Chapter Seven: The Dawn of a Bright New Morning 86
    Chapter Eight: One Big Mistake. 95
    Chapter Nine: Prophecies of Disaster 100
    Chapter Ten: Gathering Clouds 107
    Chapter Eleven: The Storm Breaks. 111
PART V: Manasseh, the King. 117
    Chapter Twelve: Wait on the Lord 118
An Outline of Isaiah. 123
Additional Sources. 138

Acknowledgements

The decision I made to leave all my local duties behind and go to Thailand for two months proved just the nudge I needed to concentrate on writing. It was a wonderful day when I finished the story of Isaiah.

Many people have helped me get to this point. My husband, most of all, has always encouraged me to stop whatever else I was doing and write. He didn't quite understand how hard that was. Then, living in a small apartment with only three suitcases of belongings and a handy cafeteria—so I didn't have to cook even once in two months—did the trick. But I also thank Charlie and Carolyn Webb, Galen and Luci Kelm, and Marilyn Justesen for their faith in me and their encouragement.

In Thailand, friends from long ago and new friends we had just met were endlessly helpful—Soraj, Tom, and June, and Siroj whom we had known since the early '80s in Singapore took wonderful care of us. Wayne Hamra and his wife also went out of their way to make our stay pleasant. I especially thank Pradeep and Nola Tudu for a hundred kindnesses. Damien Ginajil, the university librarian gave me access to books I could not have otherwise found. His wife, Teresa, cooked delicious food that cheered our hearts. His associate, Weerakoon Suwiboonsup, saw to it that we could always take books home even though we didn't have a library card.

Once the manuscript was complete, Dr. Kham Khai and Nola Tudu were the first readers to give me an indication how the story would come across to someone other than Calvin and me. Their enthusiasm was very encouraging. Calvin had listened intently as chapter by chapter the book had evolved, but other input than his was necessary to get an unprejudiced perspective. Marilyn

Bennett Justesen, Andrea Kristensen, Bernie Stepke, Dee Gregory, George and Bonnie Knight, Patricia Brown, and Tom and Bonnie Sanford, are friends who read and critiqued the manuscript for me. My thanks to all of them. Especially Bonnie Sanford who not only read but edited and gave me lots of helpful suggestions. This book is better because of her.

Most of all, I thank the Lord who always fulfills His promises. "LORD, you establish peace for us; all that we have accomplished you have done for us" (Isa. 26:12).

Introduction

You are reading this book because perhaps you have at least a passing interest in the prophets of the Old Testament. Maybe you have more than once gotten lost in Isaiah's seemingly endless chapters of complaints about the misbehaviors of God's people and their neighbors.

I believe the information you find here will help you see that Isaiah's complaints were based on real situations that confronted God's people. Fortunately, archaeology and secular history, as well as the Bible, have brought political and cultural events to light in such a way that we now know Isaiah could have been writing the newspaper headlines and lead stories of his day.

Of course, there are aspects of Isaiah's life that no historical evidence reveals. In those cases, in order to flesh out the story, you will find fictionalizations of how it might have happened. For instance, Isaiah was born and grew up during the reign of King Uzziah, but the Bible doesn't tell us anything about that until Isaiah sees God in the year that Uzziah died. My very literary and creative granddaughter, Jessica Dill, has helped me enormously with captivating creations that fill in those gaps. Many times, these are mixed in with Bible information about the various kings in the Old Testament books of 2 Kings and 2 Chronicles. You can know for sure what is invented and what is true (from the Bible) if you read the section on each of the kings as they are introduced in the narrative. Be sure to notice that 2 Kings tells about the kings of both Israel and Judah, while 2 Chronicles has only the stories about the kings of Judah.

Please remember that the purpose of these fictionalizations is always to help you grasp that Isaiah was a real person—as real as you are—with problems and perplexities in his life, just as you have in your life. God was always guiding him, as He wants to guide you. And because Isaiah was faithful to the task that God gave him, he has provided lots of wonderful encouragement and inspiration for each of us in his writings. That is why his book is often called the "Fifth Gospel." It contains so much about the life of Jesus—although in prophetic form—that it fits well with the New Testament books of Matthew, Mark, Luke, and John in showing us who Jesus was, why He came to this earth, and how He represented His Father.

Back when I was a pre-teen, I would feel compelled to read the Bible through every year. I'm not sure who put that pressure on me—whether it was my parents, teachers, or the pastor—maybe nobody did. But I loved above all things to read, so I would try. By Leviticus, I was losing steam and would finally give up on that book. (Now that Dr. Roy Gane has written some good books on Leviticus,[1] you don't have to experience the same failure I did.) I liked history and I especially liked Proverbs for some reason, and so, as the weeks went by, I would continue through the Old Testament. But then I would come to Isaiah and become downright depressed. Jeremiah and Ezekiel were much the same. Daniel, at least the first half of the book, was great. And then there were all those other little books. I don't remember whether I ever actually finished reading the Bible straight through or not!

As time went by though, I came to love Bible study more and more, and I looked for ways that the books of the Bible could help me to figure out my problems. When I was the Children's Ministries Director at the General Conference from 1989 to 2003, I led many seminars with activities that helped make sense of the Bible. No one learned more than I did! For example, you can gain lots of insights by paying attention to the generations of people that lived before the flood. When you figure out who could have been Ezra's friends, you begin to see how many of the minor prophets, as well as other famous Bible people, overlapped in time and probably, or definitely, knew each other. Maybe you have already participated in some of the activities, as found in *Making the Bible a Delight*[2] that I wrote with my friend Sally Dillon.

Finally, I came to the place where I was ready to tackle Isaiah. To my surprise, when I checked his chapters with Bible commentaries, there in black and white were the reasons why he wrote what he did. I was so inspired by what I found that I definitely wanted to share that knowledge. After a couple of years of research and note-taking, it was time to create the manuscript. In order to

---

1 Roy Gane, *Leviticus, Numbers—The NIV Application Commentary* (Grand Rapids, MI: Zondervan, 2004).

2 Sally Dillon and Virginia Smith, *Making the Bible a Delight! A Guide to Bible Study with Children* (Hagerstown, MD: Review and Herald Graphics, 1997).

have time to write, I came to Thailand where I finished this manuscript. I hope you can soon read it and be as inspired by Isaiah as I, and countless others, have been.

After you read this book, please send a letter or an email to the publishing house to let me know if this book was helpful. Did it make you want to read the Bible more? Did it make Isaiah seem more real to you than before? Would you like a similar book that focuses on the life of Jeremiah, Ezekiel, or Daniel?

Virginia L. Smith
Asia-Pacific International University
Muak Lek, Thailand
January to March 2020

PART I:

Uzziah and the Time of Prosperity[3]

---

[3] The Bible stories from the time of King Uzziah and his father, King Amaziah, are taken from 2 Kings 14:1–22; 15:1–7; and 2 Chronicles 25 and 26.

Chapter One:
Prologue

It was the height of the battle. The zing of flying arrows, yells, shouts, and groans filled the air. Dust hung so heavily that it was hard to make out specific details. The smell of blood was everywhere. Although the Philistines were losing, they weren't giving up yet. Suddenly one of their fighters saw an opportunity to kill King Uzziah, who was co-regent with his father King Amaziah[4] of Judah. Raising his bow, he prepared to shoot an arrow. Amoz, a sharp-eyed soldier of Judah detected his intent and instantly rushed in to protect the king. He took the arrow in his leg. Other soldiers finished off the

---
4 "Uzziah," Wikipedia, https://1ref.us/1ug (accessed May 2, 2021).

Prologue

Philistine, then carried Amoz off the field of battle. His femur was shattered. Never again would he be more than a cripple.

That evening in his headquarters tent, King Uzziah sat talking with his advisors. For the first time, he heard how close he had come to losing his life. He had seen nothing of the danger at the time. He asked who the man was who saved his life. It wasn't anyone important. Nobody knew his name until inquiries were sent throughout the camp. Even when the name *Amoz* was discovered, the king and his advisors had never heard of hm. Nevertheless, King Uzziah did not take that act of bravery lightly. Going to where the wounded lay, the king found someone to help him search for Amoz. Seating himself on the wounded man's litter, Uzziah took Amoz' hand and thanked him for his courage and bravery. Before going back to his tent, King Uzziah instructed those caring for the wounded to take particular care of Amoz. As long as the army was in the field, King Uzziah went daily to check on Amoz' condition. When the war was over and the army returned home, King Uzziah insisted on taking Amoz to the palace to complete his healing.

No longer able to fight or even to farm for the rest of his life, Amoz would have to find some sedentary job. King Uzziah continued to visit Amoz and talked to him about what he could possibly do. Their time together allowed them to become quite friendly. King Uzziah discovered that this man was cheerful and optimistic and could even be amusing. One day, Amoz revealed that he had always loved to read. For his time and position in society, that was unusual. It gave the king the idea of training him to be a court reporter. Amoz was very happy with the plan and applied himself diligently to the task.

* * * * *

Anyah yawned, stretched and wished she could go back to sleep. Why in the world should she wake up? This day would be as useless and boring as all the rest of her days. She, who was the youngest sister of King Amaziah, the youngest daughter of King Joash, and the pet and darling of the palace, now had to deal with boredom. How could this have happened? Life had been perfect until she was thirteen, when her brother decided she should get married. What a horrible thought. And what a horrible man he had chosen for her! He wasn't even royal! Just somebody her brother wanted to honor for some inscrutable reason. Thinking about it now, with a bitter taste in her mouth, she realized she should have asked him to explain to her his reasons. Maybe if she had understood, things might have turned out better. Suddenly she was expected to stop playing with her pet animals, her girlfriends, and her jewelry. Instead, she must embroider, and sew clothes. Who in their right mind sewed clothes? And the servants began to teach her all the duties she would be expected to perform for a husband. Yuck! She didn't want a husband, and she certainly wasn't interested in changing her privileged life. Her mother was sympathetic, but assured her that every girl, no matter who her family was, had to accept a marriage arranged by her father or brother. During that year, Anyah wept and complained and struggled to avoid cooperating with any of the wedding plans. As soon as she had her fourteenth birthday, the wedding took place. It was all a nightmare.

Fortunately, it didn't last long. The man sent her home saying she was too spoiled to be his wife. All she ever did was throw temper tantrums. She was more than happy to be back in her own palace rooms. Again, she could do whatever she wanted and just enjoy life.

* * * * *

King Uzziah had his days filled with matters of state. His father, King Amaziah, was ineffective. He had never gotten over his disastrous war with Israel which resulted in the loss of the treasures from the kingdom as well as the tearing down of six hundred feet of Jerusalem's wall. The people of Judah never forgave him. To make matters worse, he continued to worship the gods of Edom that he had brought back with him after he defeated ten thousand Edomites and captured Sela by the Dead Sea.[5] A prophet (we are not told which one) came and said to him, "Why would you expect them to help you, when they couldn't even save their own people against you?"[6] Somehow or other, Amaziah's mind was too dull to grasp the logic of that question, and he continued worshipping idols with dire results. Some years later he was assassinated.

Altogether, King Uzziah served twenty-three years as co-ruler with his father. It was during these years that he changed his name.[4] Originally, he was King Azariah, but the high priest was also named Azariah. He thought it best to avoid confusion and take a different name. Although he was only sixteen when he began to reign, he was godly and conscientious. He determined by God's help to undo the damage his father had caused and make the kingdom what God wanted it to be.

---

5   As described in 2 Kings 14:7 and 2 Chron. 25:11.
6   As described in 2 Chron. 25:14, 15.

Prologue

As the years went by, it was not just matters of state that concerned King Uzziah. In his father's place he also had to settle issues within his extended family. The women, especially, seemed to have more than their share of conflicts and tension. Those who had children got along better because they were busier, unless there was jealousy over someone else's children. Those without children had too much time on their hands and too little responsibility in their lives. One of the major problems was his aunt Anyah, his father's youngest sister. By now she was nearly 30 years old, far past marriageable age, and had long been considered unsuitable for remarriage. Her tempestuous personality meant she had always gotten her own way, except for the brief period of her marriage, and she certainly had no intentions of backing down now. Many people inside and outside the palace disliked her. King Uzziah realized that she was a special case to be handled carefully for politics sake as well as for her own well-being.

Family members complained to him that she stormed through the palace, taking whatever she wanted and demanding that others submit to her wishes. They considered her a tyrant. She did have a group of so called friends outside the palace who also were unmarried women. They loved fashion and parties and gambling, and not much else. With such a shallow life, Anyah did not feel very good about herself or others. Nobody in the palace wanted to associate with her.

King Uzziah thought deep and hard about what he could do with her or for her. He was sure he couldn't change her. Somehow, he needed to give her responsibility for something that would take her in a new direction and, hopefully, give a deeper meaning to her life. He thought about the problem so much that he even started dreaming about her. In one of his dreams, he saw Anyah heavy with child and fussing about how uncomfortable she was. But did he maybe catch a glimpse of a momentary smile on her face? With a start, Uzziah woke up and decided what to do. He determined that there could be no way for Anyah to counter his plan.

*****

Anyah was pleasantly surprised to receive a summons from her nephew, King Uzziah. What in the world could he want? She had never been called to visit with him before, and she had seldom even seen him except at a family meal now and then. She was intrigued. At last, something interesting was happening in her day. She dressed carefully and hurried to her appointment. Uzziah greeted her kindly, asking questions about what she was finding to do with her life, and listening attentively to her answers. Because of his respectful attitude, she found herself expressing to him her dissatisfaction with life. She admitted that she was bored. Her friends were only interested in her because she was a member of the royal family. They always expected something in return for their friendship, either money or some kind of useful contact.

When a break came in the conversation, King Uzziah told his aunt he thought he had found a solution for her. He had the perfect place for her at court. The thought of actually having a position in the court raised her hopes higher than they had been for a long time. What could her nephew possibly have in mind? She would soon know. King Uzziah invited her to come with him. They walked to an area of the palace where she had never been, where the historians worked, keeping track of the events taking place in the kingdom.

They stopped before a common-looking crippled man. What could they be doing here? How could she, a member of the royal family, have anything to do with this place, with this person? King Uzziah soon dispelled her wonderment. He introduced her to Amoz, who had saved his life and who was going to marry her. It was hard to tell whether Amoz or Anyah was more shocked. Anyah exploded in anger and refused to even consider such a thing. King Uzziah flatly told her she had no say in the matter. He had decided on this, and his father, her brother, had agreed. She hadn't found anything else to do with her life, so now she would be the wife of this man whom the king delighted to honor.

King Uzziah dismissed her to prepare for the marriage which would take place later that day. Then he spent time talking to Amoz about Anyah's background, so that he would know what he was getting into and why the king wished it. He thought Amoz' sense of humor would carry him through, and Uzziah was pleased with the means he had found of incorporating him into the royal family. Next, he assigned the servants who would surround the couple and make sure there would be no possibility of Anyah finding a way of escape. Finally, he issued an official statement to the extended royal family ordering them to attend the wedding and rejoice with the new couple. There was a lot of laughing in the women's apartments that afternoon.

* * * * *

"Take him away. I don't even want to see him," said his mother when her baby was born.

"Give him to me. I'm taking care of him," said his father, Amoz. "His name shall be Isaiah, meaning *Jehovah is Salvation*. He is to always be at my side."

And sure enough, Isaiah spent the first seventeen years of his life almost entirely by his father's side. Amoz even took the baby to work with him. Later he taught Isaiah to read and write, and together they studied the scrolls of the Holy Scriptures. His mother bitterly laughed at the two of them for their seriousness. She said she had better things to do, although it was hard to see what that might have been. She never seemed to be usefully employed doing anything.

There was one lapse in his friendship with his father. The year Isaiah turned thirteen, his mother tried for a time to get closer to him. Wanting more influence over him, in order to keep him from going to work with his father, she arranged appointments for him with the sons of families she knew. At first he thought it was fun, and Anyah was delighted. Then one day Isaiah told her one of his friends was going to the pagan temple. Anyah encouraged Isaiah to go along and see what it was like. She also went, but secretly, because she wanted to watch his reactions. He was too smart for that and spotted her immediately. Halfway through the activities, he came and said, "Let's get out of here."

> *Isaiah spent the first seventeen years of his life almost entirely by his father's side. Amoz even took the baby to work with him. Later he taught Isaiah to read and write, and together they studied the scrolls of the Holy Scriptures.*

"What's the matter?" Anyah asked. "Do you want to be a spoilsport and lose your friends?

"I will choose my own friends. Frankly, I prefer a God who is kind and logical, not cruel and silly. I will never come here again!"

"Have some respect for your mother and don't talk to me like that!"

Instantly, Isaiah replied impudently, "Have some respect for my father, then I will have respect for you!" She couldn't think of a good rebuttal, so both of them were silent as they continued home.

Anyah realized she had lost her chance to run his life. Nevertheless, she pondered how a thirteen-year-old boy could think like that and be so decisive. Weren't friends supposed to be more influential than anyone else at that age? He was far different from what she had been at thirteen.

* * * * *

Amoz was relieved and happy to have Isaiah back with him in the court. As he grew up in the palace, Isaiah learned the social graces and refined speaking patterns of the royal household. Over the years, he developed into a tall and handsome aristocrat. Anyah began to see that he was some good to her after all. Even as she reveled in the complements she received about her son, to her shock she realized that he probably resembled Amoz when he had been a strong healthy young military man. Very early in her marriage, Anyah had taken charge of Amoz' wardrobe, so he immediately stopped looking like a common laborer, but that was about as far as she had gone to influence his life. Now, new regard for this man she had lived with for years began to grow slowly in her mind.

Isaiah was now the age at which Jewish boys were expected to become engaged to a thirteen-year-old girl of their parents' choosing, and then, after one year, to marry. Anyah was amused by young girls who suddenly wanted to be friendly with her. She heard them whisper to each other that he would be perfect if only he weren't so serious. She observed the admiring looks he received from her relatives and acquaintances—especially from all the marriageable girls and their parents. She began to plot the most advantageous marriage she could imagine. The girl needed to be beautiful and rich and well connected, someone who would advance Anyah's status even though she was not married to a royal. At least she was a royal herself, and Amoz had a high position in the government. Plus, he was one of the closest men to King Uzziah. That counted for a lot.

Anyah thought she knew just the girl. Her name was Janeena. At twelve years of age, she looked like an angel. That provided a few months for Anyah to plan her strategy. The girl's parents were prominent in business and social circles. Just the kind of people with whom Amoz would never have anything in common. Never mind, she would find a way.

Amoz also had Isaiah's marriage on his mind. His health had suffered from the lingering effects of the injury, and he did not expect to live very much longer. Hopefully, he could find a wife as well as a career for his son before he died. There were certainly no limits to the willing candidates to be Isaiah's wife. Hardly a week went by that a father of a thirteen-year-old girl did not come to consult him about the possibility of a match between their children.

The close bond between father and son acquired through all the years they spent together made them very close friends. Also, Amoz recognized his son's intelligence and love for God. He could be trusted to offer his own advice on the various candidates for matrimony. Every girl whose name was presented was turned down by Isaiah. One after another—they were too young, too foolish, too thoughtless, too something. Isaiah's wife would have to be a very special girl. Could such a one even be found in the kingdom for this young man who was now nineteen years old?

Months passed, and Janeena had her thirteenth birthday. The special celebration was attended by the cream of Jerusalem's society. Anyah managed to get an invitation. This was her element. She loved being with all these successful people. No matter that a family idol stood in the corner of the room. She was more than familiar with such things. The birthday girl sat like a statue throughout the party. Anyah remembered her feelings at thirteen in just such a setting. This little girl didn't look any more eager than Anyah had felt. What kind of a wife would she make? It really didn't matter. After the first few weeks, husbands weren't around very much. They had their own lives to live. Janeena was rich enough to have servants to do all the work that needed to be done. She would find some way to entertain herself.

Off on the edges of the crowd were the sons of the party-goers. They were having fun with a party of their own, but Anyah could see that they were stealing glances at Janeena. Anyah stole glances at them, sizing up the competition. Isaiah was at least as tall as any of them. He was way more handsome, at least in her estimation. But somehow, he looked different from any of them. She mused over that as the evening progressed. What was it that made her son look unlike any of those boys? They reminded her of boys she had liked when she was twelve and thirteen. Happy, joking, even silly boys. It began to sink in that Isaiah was different because he was more like a man than a boy. He hadn't grown up playing with kids his age. He had grown up with his father, living in a world of grown-up working men. No wonder girls complained that he was too serious. He was serious. Anyah actually liked him the way he was. She thought he had the best chance of anyone to marry into this distinguished family. Since Amoz would be hopeless at doing the negotiation, she would ask King Uzziah to approach Janeena's father. He had arranged her marriage. He owed it to her to arrange her son's marriage. That was the perfect plan. How could anyone refuse the king?

Chapter Two:
Isaiah, the Young Man[7]

A career for Isaiah was easier to nail down. Through the years King Uzziah had never forgotten what Amoz did for him. They saw each other often and never failed to find something interesting to talk about. Uzziah was aware of how sadly the marriage between Amoz and Anyah had turned out. Yet, they did stay together. At first, Uzziah had guaranteed it by the staff he assigned to work for them. As the years went by, Anyah could have left if she had wanted to, but somehow the marriage and the child ultimately provided something she had found lacking in her life. Uzziah had not failed to notice their wonderful son and was gratified that he could be a member of the royal family. He never missed an opportunity to tell Anyah that Isaiah was growing into a valuable member of the court.

Now, knowing that his time was short, Amoz presumed to send a message, asking the king to visit him in their apartment. Only the urgency he felt prompted him to request such a visit. When King Uzziah arrived, he was shocked to see his friend in bed, looking very frail. Isaiah had been sent off on an errand, so the two men were alone. Concealing his concern, King Uzziah asked Amoz what was on his mind. Amoz' appeal was that Isaiah be allowed to take over his job as court reporter. For years, Isaiah had been helping his father work, so he knew the job well. The proud father said that his son could

---

7   The stories of Queen Athaliah and King Joash come from 2 Kings, chapters 11 and 12; 2 Chronicles 22:10–12 and chapters 23 and 24.

do a better job than he ever had. He saw that Isaiah had a great gift with words. He felt sure the boy's intelligence came more from the royal side of the family than from his. Uzziah laughed at that and countered that the available evidence showed that it came largely from the father. The king readily agreed that the two should continue working together until Amoz could not continue. Then Isaiah should take over where Amoz had left off. Neither man mentioned death, but it was clear to see that Amoz was weakening. When the visit was over, the king assigned two more servants to care for Amoz and be sure that he had everything he needed.

As the next few months passed, Anyah made it a point to stop by Amoz' room once a day to visit for five minutes or so and ask if he needed anything. That was as close as she had ever come to apologizing for all the years of ignoring and belittling him, but he appreciated the effort she was making.

His father rested in death before Isaiah turned twenty. The two of them had been so close knit for years that Isaiah mourned his father's passing for a very long time. He would never cease to take pride in his father and referred to himself over and over as the son of Amoz. Anyah was happy that she was now the only one with the responsibility of choosing a wife for her son. A few months before, when she had asked King Uzziah to negotiate for Janeena, he had laughed at her. Aware of the girl's character, he pointed out that Anyah was trying to set up her son for the same kind of marriage she had had the first time. Did she really want to do that? Probably not. With nowhere else to turn, she dropped the idea.

Despite her best efforts, Isaiah proved to be an exceptionally difficult young man for whom to find a wife. Having learned from Amoz that a marriage would not happen if Isaiah did not agree, she presented the name of one girl after another, but Isaiah was very resistant. If a disagreement between mother and son became too forceful—usually because the potential bride's family was offering a large dowry that Anyah wanted to get her hands on—Isaiah would speak to his cousin, King Uzziah. Immediately word would come that this marriage was not allowed by the king.

Isaiah soon became an outstanding historian of the events of King Uzziah's reign. A year passed quickly. It was a pleasure for Isaiah to go to the palace every morning and sit in on all the king's consultations so he could accurately write down what had taken place. King Uzziah was a righteous man, eager to make decisions that were right for the kingdom as well as right in God's eyes. Frequently, he would remind his counselors that God was the actual king of Judah. He, Uzziah, was merely the errand boy. And the evidence showed that, as long as he maintained such a humble attitude, God gave him success. His reign, espe-

Isaiah, the Young Man

cially when he alone was king after his father was murdered (2 Kings 14:19–20; 2 Chron. 25:27–28), was a time of exceptional prosperity. He repaired what had been damaged during his father's time. He regained the territory that had been lost. He greatly strengthened the military power of Judah and beautified Jerusalem. The city had not looked so good since the time of King Solomon.

As part of his job, Isaiah studied the past rulers of Judah and understood that righteous behavior had often been in short supply. The fact that they were his ancestors gave him an intense interest in learning about their lives. His great-great-grandmother Athaliah had grabbed the throne when her son King Ahaziah was killed (2 Kings 9:22–28), and then had done her best to kill off every male member of the royal family descended from King David (2 Kings 2:11). Fortunately, Jehosheba,[8] the aunt of those who were being killed, but not the daughter of Athaliah (2 Chron. 22:11), was married to Jehoiada a righteous priest. She had the same father as the king who had been killed, but she had a different mother. She managed to steal away Joash the youngest son of the dead king. She and her husband hid him in the temple for six years while they prepared him to be king and taught him how to live for God (2 Kings 11:2).

Meanwhile, Athaliah ruled the country and built a temple to Baal filled with altars and idols. She hired priests of Baal to be the chief spiritual leaders in Jerusalem. It was too dangerous to disagree with her, so most people went along with her commands. Those who didn't go along, stayed very quiet and prayed that God would somehow return the city to righteous rulers.

At last, the time was right. A growing number of the people were sick and tired of Athaliah's rulership. Jehoiada secretly made agreements with military chiefs who discretely gathered all the Levites and the heads of Israelite families from all the towns. Sabbath morning came, the day when Athaliah was least likely to show up at the temple. Jehoiada gave instructions to each group as to where they should stand and what they should do. Little King Joash was brought out by Jehoiada and his sons, a crown was put on his head, and he was presented with a copy of the books of the law written by Moses.

Then they anointed his head with oil and shouted, "Long live the king." Crowds of people were running and shouting and cheering. God had remembered them! Athaliah heard the deafening noise and came to see what was happening. What she saw was little King Joash, flanked by trumpeters, choirs singing praise songs, and crowds of people rejoicing. She tore her robes and shouted, "Treason! Treason!" Because Jehoiada had so well organized the

---

8   Ellen G. White, *Prophets and Kings,* (Mountain View, CA: Pacific Press Publishing Association, 1943), 371.1. See also "Jehosheba," Wikipedia, https://1ref.us/1uh (accessed May 2, 2021).

groups, they had no problem in capturing Athaliah and taking her away from the temple to be killed. Anyone who sided with her would get the same treatment. Next the leaders tore down the temple to Baal, smashed the altars and idols, and killed the priests of Baal.

Jehoiada then presented a covenant that he and the people and the new King Joash would sign, agreeing to be the Lord's people. All the years that Jehoiada lived and led out in the temple services, King Joash followed God. Isaiah was happy that his great grandfather Joash had had so many good years. When Jehoiada, the priest, died at the age of 130, he was buried with the kings of Judah in honor of how much he had done for the kingdom and the temple.

Unfortunately, with Jehoiada out of the way, King Joash's advisors persuaded him to abandon the temple of God and worship at the pagan Asherah poles and idols[9] instead. God sent messengers to try to bring the kingdom of Judah back to true worship, but they were rejected.

Then God sent a message through Zechariah, son of Jehoiada the priest. If they persisted in disobeying the Lord's commands, they would not prosper. Danger and destruction lay ahead for them. Isaiah cringed when he read that it was King Joash himself who gave the order for Zechariah to be stoned to death. How could he have forgotten all the kindness of Jehoiada who had been a father to him?

The very next year, a small army from Aram invaded, killed the leaders of Jerusalem and Judah, and sent all the treasure that was plundered to their king in Damascus. King Joash was left severely wounded. His officials conspired against him because he had killed Zechariah, and they killed him as he lay wounded in his bed. After 38 righteous years of ruling, King Joash had ruined everything by abandoning God. He died at the young age of 47.

Isaiah was interested to read about the two men who dealt out King Joash's judgment. They were named, and their mothers were named, but not their fathers. One mother was an Ammonite, and the other was a Moabite, both descended from Lot, Abraham's nephew. Their sons were officials in the court of King Joash, so it was clear that there were still people, even from the extended family of Abraham, who knew right from wrong. They were willing to risk their lives to defend what was right.

Isaiah hoped and prayed that King Uzziah would stay close to God and continue to have a successful reign without turning from God and allowing evil to guide his mind. Neither he nor his father, King Amaziah, had destroyed the high places or the Asherah poles where the people loved to worship idols and

---

9 "Asherah pole," Wikipedia, https://1ref.us/1ui (accessed May 2, 2021).

play. There was evidence that God could not bless His people as abundantly as He wished to when they were dividing their worship between Him and pagan gods. The streets of Jerusalem were often the scene of violence and crime. Isaiah felt sure that had to be examples of the fact that God's blessing could not be given in its fullness.

After seventeen years of ruling alone, King Uzziah decided it was time to make his son Jotham co-ruler with him. Many in the government, Isaiah included, were not so sure this was a good idea. Everyone could see that Jotham was leading the life of a rich indolent playboy. If he had responsibilities now, Uzziah hoped that would prepare him for the time when he would be the sole ruler. As a result, there was a huge coronation that took most of a year to plan. Because of its importance to the history of Uzziah's reign, Isaiah was often involved with the preparations. By the time Jotham's coronation had taken place, Isaiah was twenty-one years old.

In his free time, Isaiah liked nothing better than to study Scripture scrolls with men who feared God and shunned the typical idolatrous worship practices and entertainments of Jerusalem. One of them, Ruel, was the most spiritual man Isaiah had ever met. The companionship of these men helped fill the deep void in Isaiah's life after his father died. Every time they were together, Isaiah was blessed by their conversation and the reading and prayers they shared. It provided the perfect counterpart to the secular environment that took up most of Isaiah's days. Together he and Ruel frequently mourned over the lack of spirituality within Judah. The temple was busy with all the usual rituals, but the lives of many of the people performing those rituals were anything but righteous.

Isaiah's own mother went to the temple every day, but it seemed like it was mostly so she could see who was there and be sure she was wearing a better garment than anyone else. She claimed it was her responsibility to enhance the honor of the royal family. In addition, she was also going to worship idols at the high places. She was perfectly happy with pagan gods. She said they were more fun, and that was where she met the friends she liked the best. Her flippant attitude sickened Isaiah, but he had long since known that he could not change her. They lived in the same apartment in the palace, but their lives hardly touched. Isaiah and Ruel often discussed how patient God had been with His chosen people, and how they imposed on His goodness while engaging in sinful practices.

Even the children were affected. Once, as Isaiah left Ruel's house, he found an unruly group of children outside. They were laughing and yelling and punching someone. Striding over to the middle of the group, he found that a young woman was the one being tormented. She looked like she was at least thirteen or fourteen years old. He quickly pulled her away from the crowd and commanded the rest in no uncertain terms to leave her alone and go home. Considering what she had just been through, she was amazingly calm. Inquiring where her home was, Isaiah heard to his surprise that she was Ruel's daughter. As he walked her to the front door, he asked her what had happened.

"Oh, they just like to tease me because I get messages. They don't really hurt me."

"What kind of messages do you get?"

"Sometimes God tells me to encourage someone or, once in a while, to warn someone."

"How do you know it is God telling you?"

"I just know because it has happened a bunch of times."

Ruel came to the door, took his daughter inside and thanked Isaiah for helping her. Then he shut the door. On his way home, Isaiah pondered what he had seen and heard. He wondered why Ruel had never mentioned the girl or her messages.

The next time Ruel and Isaiah were studying together, he asked about the messages. Ruel looked embarrassed. He said he and his wife were not sure what to make of them and were afraid something was wrong with their daughter's mind.

Isaiah asked, "Do you see bad results from her messages?"

"No, I can't say we do. In fact, several years ago when she was really young, she told me I needed to study the scrolls and that was when I started reading."

"She told me God gives her the messages."

"Yes," Ruel replied. "That is what she always says."

"But you aren't so sure?"

"Well, it is more complicated than that. It is an impossible thought that God might have put a prophetess in my humble house. It just could not be true."

Isaiah lightly disagreed, "But of course anything is possible. It will be interesting to see what happens to her and her messages as she grows older."

"Yes, I suppose so," her father said hesitantly.

"Meanwhile, isn't she marriageable age?"

Again, Ruel hesitated. "According to the customs of our people she is, but my wife and I have decided not to arrange a marriage for her because she may not be mentally sound. She is a good girl who can stay home and continue to help us as we get older."

Isaiah, the Young Man

"You as her parents would know best." Isaiah finished, and the two men turned to the scrolls.

* * * * *

One day, some months later, as Isaiah approached their apartment, his mother met him at the door crying. He didn't remember ever seeing her cry before. He was unsure what to do. Should he hug her? Should he pretend not to see and ignore her? As it turned out, there was no ignoring her. He was the reason she was crying.

She pulled him inside the door, slammed it shut, and sat him down on the nearest bench. Then she exploded, "You seem so pious, but you really are a naughty boy! People are talking about you…"

When Isaiah was able to get a word in edgewise, he queried, "What in the world are you saying? I have no idea what anyone could be complaining about. I am busy at my work, and I do little else."

"But you spend time with men I don't know," his mother sobbed. "Men who are outside the palace."

"Well, it's true I study the scrolls with some righteous men I have met in the city," Isaiah acknowledged.

"How would anybody know they are righteous? How would anyone know you are spending time studying the scrolls?" she asked accusingly.

"Why would we be doing anything else," Isaiah questioned, confused by her lack of logic.

"People are asking me why you aren't married. They are suggesting something is wrong with you." Now Anyah was crying hard again.

The light began to dawn as Isaiah watched his mother closely. He could see this was a new ploy to try and bend him to her will. How many times had she tried to find him a wife? The problem was that her idea of his wife was not his idea of his wife. Maybe he could figure out a way to pacify her without letting her choose for him. Isaiah was not against getting married. He just did not want the kind of wife his mother would find.

Isaiah stood up, which caused his mother to quiet down as she wondered what he was about to do. He spoke, "All right, I see that it is terribly important to you that I get married. Let me go to the king and ask him to choose a wife for me. He was the one who arranged your marriage. He can do the same for me."

"I don't know," she hedged. She could see that this would keep her from choosing her daughter-in-law. "He didn't do so well for me. Are you sure you will be willing to accept the wife he chooses?"

"As a result of your marriage, I am your son. Is there someone else you would rather have as a son?"

"No," she admitted. "You are a good son." Tears turned to pouting as she realized that once again her plan was foiled. Here she had the most handsome son and the one with the most power at court, but she couldn't find any way to control him. He was always beyond her reach. She prayed and prayed to the gods to help her manage his life and make him popular with her associates, but the gods never seemed to hear her prayers.

* * * * *

"Please convey my regards to King Uzziah. I request a private audience with him at his convenience."

"Of course, Isaiah, I'm sure he will send you a message when you can see him," responded the court official with a bow.

Even though Isaiah sat in on the morning conferences and knew all the state secrets, he seldom actually visited with his cousin, the king. The personal nature of the request he planned to present meant that this visit had to be a private one. Because the king was actively involved in projects all over the kingdom, it could be some time before he would be able to fit in a personal interview with Isaiah who was happy to wait. Now that he had found a way around his mother's incessant attempts to find him a wife, he was happy to lay aside that subject and continue to concentrate on his career.

Isaiah loved to fit words into powerful, beautiful language. As he wrote his notes on the events of the day, he was not satisfied to just use whatever words would convey the meaning. Instead, he labored over the words he would use and how he would arrange them. Sometimes he was accused good naturedly of writing poetry instead of history. But his history was sound. Nobody complained that he was making a report that was not true. It was reporting that read so well that it was memorable and pleasing to the ear. His grammar was perfect, despite the fact that he had received all of his education in the history section of the palace. Many of the men he worked around were well-educated. From them, he learned the elegant sound of the court language and how to write it appropriately. And then he perfected it more than anyone else. It was clear that he had been destined for this job.

It was weeks before his cousin called him to his private apartment. King Uzziah well respected this young man who made such a contribution to his government. The fact that he was a member of the royal family just added to his already stellar reputation. King Uzziah waited eagerly to hear what Isaiah had come to request.

"Your Majesty, may you live forever," began Isaiah.

"Oh, come on. We are family members. Why so formal?" asked the king.

"I never want to impose on your kindness which has already been great to my family. And I'm afraid that this time I may be imposing."

"What can I do for you? I'm sure it is something we can work out. By the way, how is your mother?"

"She is fine. The same way she's always been."

Uzziah laughed, "I think I understand that."

Isaiah continued, "You have helped me out several times when she was determined to arrange a marriage for me with someone unsuitable. Now I have told her I would ask you to arrange my marriage. That way I don't have to fight with her anymore over her unfortunate choices."

Uzziah looked grave. "I know it was your father's deepest wish to live long enough to see you happily married. What did he say to you on the subject?"

Isaiah looked a little bashful as he admitted that his father always asked his advice, even though it was totally contrary to the usual practice.

"And he never suggested someone you could seriously consider?"

"I tried to seriously consider all of them, just because he talked to me about them. But none of them interested me."

"What makes you think I can do any better than your father?"

Now Isaiah looked really embarrassed. "Maybe I have found someone who does interest me. My mother would hate the thought of this girl. But if you could give your blessing, my mother would not be able to protest."

The king smiled. "How very interesting. Do you want to tell me who she is?"

"First let me say that I have not approached her parents. They have no clue of my feelings. I didn't have a clue myself until my mother started crying and pressuring me again about the necessity of marrying. Furthermore, this girl's parents don't expect her to marry."

Then Isaiah told King Uzziah about his encounter with Ruel's daughter Yishka, and the conversation he had later with her father. He included her calmness in the face of torment and said he thought such a personality might be able to get along with his mother.

Uzziah laughed heartily. "She sounds like a very serious girl. That would certainly make her a good match for you, my serious cousin. Her name is also an appropriate one, meaning "the one who sees."

Isaiah smiled. He liked her name.

"Here is my suggestion. Continue your visits with her father. Observe anything you can that will let you know more about her. If I make inquiries, it will become public and will probably upset the parents. If you can come back and tell me that you are sure you want to marry her, I will give my blessing without hesitation. Then to satisfy your mother, I will arrange the final negotiations about the dowry."

"Oh, I don't need a dowry. My mother will want it, but I don't."

"Your wife will not feel valued without a dowry. For her sake, there needs to be one. Once you have it, you are welcome to save it for her."

"I guess that has been a neglected part of my education."

"No matter. It is those who arrange the marriage who need to know those things. You have time to learn all that before your own daughter will be old enough to marry."

Isaiah winced at such a thought.

Uzziah happily slapped him on the back. "Congratulations! We should be able to have you be a married man in a little over a year."

Feeling dazed, Isaiah walked back to his rooms. How should he manage this? He wanted to leave immediately for Ruel's house, but it wasn't the day they usually studied, so he determined to follow the routine and not give away his intentions.

Over the coming weeks Isaiah paid attention to every detail that was happening in Ruel's house. He had never done that before, and now he was trying to act naturally, but was finding it hard to do. Ruel looked at him questioningly from time to time and asked him if he was feeling well. He said he had never felt better. At last, he couldn't wait any longer. Finding himself completely alone with Ruel, he asked a series of questions.

"Do you consider me a friend?"

"Of course, I do. I consider you one of my best friends."

"Do you think of me as a trustworthy person?"

"How can you even ask such a question? With all the corruption going on in this town, how many other people besides you do I know who are trustworthy?"

"If the king should send emissaries to ask you something about me, could you promise to talk to me about it and not jump to any decision before asking me?"

"What a strange question! Isn't the king your cousin? What would he want from me?"

"You will soon know, and then we can talk directly about it."

"About what?" asked Ruel.

Isaiah, the Young Man

"You will know soon."

Ruel was mystified but began to have his suspicions while he waited for the visit. Before long, the message had gone to the king, and he had entrusted a man with the task of negotiating the marriage arrangements with the parents. They, especially the wife, were so shocked by the proposal that the man had to return a second time after Ruel and his wife had an opportunity to talk with Isaiah. Upon hearing his plea that their daughter would be the perfect wife for him, they reluctantly agreed and the arrangements began to go forward.

Once the marriage contract was about to be signed, Isaiah asked permission to visit with Yishka. She was escorted into the room, modestly keeping her eyes down. Even though she was sixteen, several years beyond the usual age for engagement, she knew what was expected of her. Isaiah began the conversation by asking her age and the order and ages of her siblings. Then he ventured to ask what her favorite foods and activities were. She solemnly answered each question, while still looking at the floor. Then he changed his tactics and mixed up the information about her sisters and waited to see if she would be confused or offended. No, instead she teased him by asking about his (nonexistent) siblings. He asked her why in the world she would want to get married when she was living in such a happy home. Her eyes twinkled as she looked up and responded by asking him why in the world he would want to get married. Now she had become more comfortable, so he became more serious. He told her he understood that her parents had not planned that she should marry, but that he had liked her from the first time they had met. He had become convinced she would make a good wife for him. Now, she had the courage to ask him some serious questions.

"What about my messages? Will that bother you?"

"No, I like the fact that you are such good friends with God that He gives you messages to deliver. I hope He will send you a message for me some day."

"I know you live at the palace and are a member of the royal family. I am a very simple girl; I don't know how to act in such a place."

"I have thought about that. We will get our own home to live in, away from the palace. This is something I especially wanted to talk to you about. I am providing your garments for the engagement party and later for the wedding. They will be very different from what you have worn before but, because I have a position in court, I ask that you wear them. Once we are in our own house you will be able to dress however you wish.

"There is something else I must tell you. Remember the day I rescued you from those mean children?"

Yishka nodded.

"I was very impressed with your calmness under those circumstances. My mother is a difficult person. She will not be pleased with our marriage. Because of what I have seen in you, I am confident you will be able to patiently bear with her strong personality. She will not be living with us, so you will not see her very often. She is the main reason why I want to provide your clothes. She is obsessed with clothing and, if you are wearing beautiful garments, she will be more likely to accept you as a worthy person.

"But no matter how she reacts to you, I greatly value you as a worthy person. You don't have to worry about how her reaction will influence me."

By this time, Yishka had turned her full attention to Isaiah's face. She wanted to tell him she would do her best to be a good wife. But as she was planning her words, a familiar feeling came over her. For a moment, she looked upward and held very still. Then she took his hand and said, "I have a message for you—and for me. God has a very special work for you to do, and I will be your helper."

The touch of her hand had sent an electric shock through Isaiah. He looked at her with new eyes and thought a year would be a long time to wait to marry her. But the time would pass, and God Himself had given them His blessing. That was beyond anything he had hoped for. When would he get to know God's plans—that special work he was to do? Never mind, in God's own time he would know.

* * * * *

The next day, three palace dressmakers arrived at Yishka's house. Isaiah had given them orders not to reveal to anyone where they were going or what they were doing. They were to prepare several outfits for Yishka and make garments for her mother and sisters as well. The household was soon in an uproar. The whole family was astonished by the fabrics, the styles, and the thought of such rich-looking clothing. Yishka hung on to the memory of Isaiah telling her he wished her to dress this way, at least until after the wedding. That evening, when Isaiah received a report, he heard that Yishka stayed calm and serene throughout the events of the day. He smiled because that was exactly what he had expected of her.

With the king's blessing, the engagement party took place in a large private hall. It was the first time Anyah had met her soon-to-be daughter-in-law. Until then, she had been in the dark about who this girl was and what kind of a family she came from. Crowds of people attended, many of whom worked with Isaiah in the palace. And, of course, all of the members of the royal family were there. Even King Uzziah made an appearance. When Anyah saw Yishka resplendent in one of her new garments, she could not help but be impressed that her son had chosen someone worthy of her royal family. She was also impressed because Yishka's whole family was so well-dressed. *The husband must be someone very important*, Anyah thought, *but who was he?* She was not able to corner Isaiah that night to ask him, so she spent the evening quite happily, satisfied with the event and the thought of a future with a stylish and beautiful daughter-in-law. This would surely be someone she could deal with.

Isaiah had almost never seen Yishka looking happy before. She hadn't looked unhappy, just solemn, but now she was radiant. For years, her life had been filled with the jeers and laughter of those who thought she was crazy. She had sadly looked forward to the long, lonely future that lay ahead while she watched other girls her age getting married and moving to their new homes. By now, she should have been already married for at least two years, but such a life was not to be for her. Amazingly, all that had changed! Now she was marrying into the royal family, marrying one of the most powerful men in the court who she knew as a kind and God-fearing person. Wearing the elegant apparel he had provided, she perceptively watched the respect and even awe dawn in the eyes of those who had formerly made fun of her. Her mother-in-law was a wild card. Yishka could not tell what she was thinking, but at least she was not unfriendly.

Isaiah found an opportunity to tell her how proud he was of her, how well she had carried herself through the ceremony. Now they had a year to make all the preparations for their life together. Only rarely could they expect to have a private moment. He had to find and prepare their house. She had to prepare the household linens and goods they would need. More garments would be readied for the marriage ceremony itself. It would be a year brimming with activity and hopes for the future.

For Isaiah, his task was not burdensome. He gave the responsibility over to the appropriate court official and returned his attention to his writing. Every few days, his agent would take him to see a house to approve or disapprove. After several unsatisfactory visits, he changed course. Finding a garden lot in a pleasant area just outside the palace grounds, he hired an experienced contractor to build a house according to his plans. From then on, it was a pleasure to walk there every evening to check on the progress. The year pass quickly, and the house with its enclosing wall was ready just in time for the marriage ceremony. The garden surrounding the house was mostly unchanged from what it had been before. He hoped Yishka would take charge of that, although he did have some suggestions to offer.

Meanwhile Anyah had managed to find out that Isaiah was marrying a girl from an unimportant family. She was furious. How dare he do such a thing and embarrass her. When she confronted him, he just laughed and said she should be happy he was marrying at all. The king had approved the marriage and she had nothing to do with it. Yishka had looked wonderful at the engagement party, so that proved she could rise to whatever level he wanted her to. He was pleased with his choice, and that was the end of the matter. Anyah was silenced for the moment, but she continued to fume.

* * * * *

A month and a half before the week-long celebration of the marriage, it was again time for the palace dressmakers to come to Ruel's house. Again, they were sworn to secrecy so no one would show up at the ceremony wearing one of the same outfits. This time the location and people involved could not be concealed. Isaiah was one of the most elegant and eligible men in the court. His height, his looks, his clothes, his aristocratic posture—all of these made him stand out in any crowd. His marriage was an event that nobody wanted to miss. Everybody who was anybody was trying to figure out a way to get an invitation.

Close to the same time, Isaiah made a point of visiting with Ruel, going over the needs for the upcoming banquet and making a generous contribution toward the food. He also introduced Ruel to a man whom he was sending to be the governor of the feast. That person would determine the menu, order the supplies, and guide the kitchen staff in food preparation. During the week of the wedding, he would also be the Master of Ceremonies and introduce each part of the program to the assembled guests. Since he also worked in the palace, he knew exactly what royalty expected during marriage feasts. Much of the stress and pressure Ruel had been feeling was relieved after that interview. Now he could relax and just be the fond father of the bride. Before they parted, Ruel and Isaiah promised each other that they would get back to studying the scrolls again just as soon as this marriage ceremony was completed. Each of them had missed the studying they had done before the house was being built, the dressmakers were in the way, and the plans for the seven daily ceremonies were being finalized. Once again, life would hopefully slow down to what had previously seemed normal.

The day came for the wedding to begin. Everything was in readiness. The bride was tall and beautiful. The groom was handsome. The decorations were worthy of the palace. The continuing feast came off without an incident. The food was delicious. Everyone who attended agreed that it was a high point of the season. Day by day, each person had played his or her part. When the various feasts and ceremonies were finally ended after seven days, Isaiah took his bride and her family to see the new home. Inwardly impatient, but without a comment, Yishka allowed everyone to go as they wished from room to room and look at everything. She waited, rejoicing in the thought that Isaiah had prepared such a nice home for her. So much better than anything she had ever dreamed of having. Then, at last, they were alone. The others had left. They could now begin their life together that they had been dreaming of for a year. They could not know at that time how many years of happy union they would have, or what God had planned for them, or what sorrows they would endure.

* * * * *

Barely two weeks after Isaiah and Yishka's marriage, there was a crisis in the palace. King Uzziah was about sixty years old—the best king by far that Judah had had in a long time and certainly the most powerful. The kingdom had greatly prospered during his reign, exceeding in size and wealth that of almost all the kings before him. During most of the time that he had been king, Uzziah had been a godly, humble man but, as his power increased, that began to subtly shift. When Isaiah was suddenly called to come immediately to the temple, he never dreamed what he would find. He rushed over only to be met by a priest who was waiting there to explain what was happening. It seemed that the king had gone mad. For some reason, he decided that he could burn incense at the altar, a task assigned by God solely to the priestly descendants of Aaron. Nobody was able to stop him from going right into the Holy Place. Through many centuries, that task had been reserved for the priests alone. Now here was the king, saying he could do whatever he wanted to!

As Isaiah arrived, the high priest determined to go in and try to dissuade King Uzziah. Eighty additional priests declared their intentions to accompany him. Surely such a crowd would have a calming effect on him. But no, instead of backing down, he became furious and raged at the priests, calling them arrogant and stiff-necked and proud. He loudly accused them of trying to usurp his power after all he had done for the country. Outside in the court of the men, Isaiah could clearly hear every word the king said. His heart sank. What he had learned from the story of King Joash had led him to pray that this would never happen to King Uzziah. Yet now it obviously had. The honor guard who had accompanied the king to the temple also heard every word and looked at each other uncomfortably.

The priests stood there, wondering what to say or what else they could do to get him to leave the Holy Place. In an instant, their problem was solved.

Eighty-one priests all at once recognized what had taken place. Leprosy had broken out on Uzziah's forehead. The shocked look on their faces made Uzziah halt his tirade. All of them were looking at his forehead, so he put his hand up and touched the swollen scaly patches that had never been there before. He recognized that God had spoken; the priests had been right in trying to remove him. Now he himself could not get out fast enough. He begged them to forgive him and pray that God would heal him. His honor guard melted away, running to the palace as fast as they could.

Outside he found only Isaiah.

"Help me, Isaiah. What should I do? Please pray that God will accept my apology and heal me."

"Yes, we will certainly pray for that. In the meantime, let me get you back to the palace before more people see you. The fewer people who know about this, the better."

Unfortunately, everybody was out and about that morning, and some of them had also heard Uzziah's words from inside the Holy Place. As they peered at the king—how often did they actually get to see their king? —they recognized the most feared disease of the time. Before King Uzziah and Isaiah could reach the palace, the news had preceded them. Guards came out to direct them—from a distance—to the back of the palace where there was an isolated garden area. There a tent was hastily put up so the king could rest in its shade. Food was brought for him and set down several yards away. Isaiah stayed with him and brought the food over for him to eat. Both men were so stunned by what had happened that they didn't know what to say. Isaiah prayed for him several times as the king wept.

After a while, King Uzziah regained his composure and called for his son Jotham so that he could consult with him on state business. Isaiah delivered the summons to a guard. As he and Uzziah waited for Jotham, Isaiah tried to comfort his cousin.

"God still loves you. Maybe He could see that this was the best way to get your attention."

"Well, He certainly has done that! Maybe I can still rule from out here in the garden."

Isaiah doubted it but didn't say so. About that time, some workmen came and began building something nearby. Then, at a distance, Isaiah saw a guard motioning to him. He went over to see what the man wanted. He handed Isaiah a message for King Uzziah from Jotham. Uzziah began weeping again as he read it.

Isaiah, the Young Man

Dear Father,

I am afraid to come to see you because our kingdom will be in danger if both of us get leprosy. It will be better for you to rest comfortably alone where you are. I have had several years of helping you reign, so I'm well prepared to carry on without you. There will be servants who will bring you food and take care of your other needs.

Your loving son,
Jotham

Isaiah was stunned by the insensitivity of the message. What kind of son would do that to his father? On the other hand, he knew the intense fear that people had of leprosy. Despite that fear, he assured Uzziah that he would return often to encourage and pray with him, although he would not touch him. Furthermore, he would bring scrolls for the stricken king to read. They would have to be burned afterwards, but that was okay.

Isaiah stayed there throughout the day and together the two of them watched the workmen build the little house where King Uzziah would spend the remaining years of his life. It was with great sadness that Isaiah finally tore himself away in the evening. He knew that Yishka would be concerned because he had been gone so long. She may have already heard what had happened.

When he reached home, to his surprise he found that Yishka was angry. He was shocked. She had never shown so much emotion. He tried to quickly explain, but she was unmoved. Finally, he told her to stay far away from him and wait to have their conversation until he had bathed and burned all the clothes he had been wearing. He added that he wasn't particularly worried about either of them getting leprosy. After all, God had sent them that special message. He was just taking precautions to protect others from fearing that he could pass on leprosy to them because he had stayed close to Uzziah.

As soon as he could, he patiently listened to Yishka complain. She had waited all day for him to get home in the evening! She had the meal ready on time! He didn't show up until the food was cold and the fire had gone out! She had barely heard that there was a problem in the palace. Why hadn't he sent her a message? He apologized profusely and answered as best he could, while thinking to himself that after two weeks of bliss, now he had to realize that marriage was not always going to be perfect. Too bad. Or was it? His new wife had real emotions that could erupt at any time. Maybe that was kind of interesting. Real life was settling in.

PART II:

Jotham, the King[10]

---
[10] The stories of King Jotham are largely drawn from 2 Kings 15:32–38 and 2 Chronicles, chapter 27.

Chapter Three:
Isaiah, the Prophet

Torn between his sympathy for King Uzziah and his wish to encourage and support King Jotham, Isaiah found himself constantly frustrated by the lack of attention to both the prevailing crime and corruption and the need for pure religion undefiled by idolatry. Nothing was being done about either one. Meanwhile, he faithfully visited Uzziah and was happy to see how much inspiration the king received from reading the scrolls. But around him, the kingdom was deteriorating.

With Jotham alone on the throne, Isaiah became more aware than ever of the sinfulness of the people of Jerusalem. With Uzziah out of sight, and especially after his bad example, it seemed that everyone felt free to do whatever seemed right in his or her own eyes. After years of being co-ruler, Jotham was a good man of twenty-five years of age, only a few years older than Isaiah. He would certainly never attempt to go into the Holy Place as his father had done. Uzziah had been right to promote him. His foolishness had ceased when he began to share the throne. He was serious now, but much inferior to his father. Whatever would make his life easier seemed to be his preferred course of action. Corruption and idolatry were running rampant in the kingdom. He did nothing to try and stop them.

Isaiah began to carry a heavy burden that he must do something since King Jotham did not. He thought of the warnings Moses had given about the results of unfaithfulness. If something were not done soon, Judah might cease to exist as a kingdom. Then what would happen to God's promise to have a descendant of David on the throne? If he personally did nothing, was there anyone else who would attempt to halt the godlessness of the city? He did not think so.

Already in his marriage he had discovered that, almost always, Yishka was a good listener. And she usually had a sound head on her that showed itself in wise counsel. He determined to talk to her about his burden. She listened intently as Isaiah explained what was happening and what he felt he needed to do about it. Her knowledge of the wickedness in the city was far less than his, but even she, as circumscribed and protected as her life had been and still was, could see that God was not being sincerely worshipped.

"Dearest husband, I believe that God is laying this burden on your mind. Because of your position and connections, you will be safe in giving a straight testimony to the people. Everyone knows you as a righteous man, so nobody will accuse you of hypocrisy. Furthermore, God has given you the gift of words. He will help you write out your message in just the language that is needed."

Her words of encouragement gave Isaiah the daring he needed to begin writing. But first he had a question for her: "How will you feel if our friends no longer want to be seen with us?"

"Such friends would be no loss to you or to me," she said promptly. "That does not worry me at all. At the very least, my father and the other men with whom you have studied the scrolls, will be happy that someone at last is speaking up for the truth.

"If our friends are truly friends, they will still like us. If not, I will find whatever friends I need. Anyway, there is always more than enough to do right here at home. Besides, I'm a little lonely for my mother and sisters. Maybe when you are busy, I will go see them more often."

"What a blessing you are to me." Isaiah smiled as he reached for her hands, relieved that his burden, which was sure to be unpopular, was not going to affect the environment of his happy home.

As he began to write, it seemed that his eyes opened ever wider to the critical situation. Yishka was right when she said God would help him with the words needed for the message. In the palace, he was familiar with legal language, and he used that to describe what God wanted to say to Judah.[11]

God has put Judah on trial. He calls on the universe as witnesses to the charges He brings. Maybe this would wake up their dull senses, and they would recognize the enormity of their transgressions. They have rebelled against Him. They care less about Him than a donkey does about its owner. The people are

---

11   You can read his full message in Isaiah, chapter 1.

laden with guilt for their corruption and evildoing. They have turned their backs on the Holy One of Israel.

Isaiah loved that phrase, *the Holy One of Israel*. That was how he constantly thought of God, and he wanted to help everyone else see God in the same way. Too many people had bought into lies about God. They thought He was heartless and harsh, a God Who was just looking to catch them doing something wrong so He could punish them. Somehow, Isaiah had to change their minds and help them understand God's great sympathy for their captive situation in a sinful world. Somehow, he had to help them see that they only had to give themselves into God's tender mercies and He would protect them and give them the best possible life for now until it was time for them to join Him forever in the better world to come.

Why would they want to continue in the same path they were following, when they were continually being beaten up, beset with injuries, and living in a desolate country that had been stripped bare and burned by enemies? The city of Jerusalem would become like a little hut in the middle of a vineyard or a melon field, a city under siege by enemies. Every other town around it would be in enemy hands. Only Jerusalem would be left free, but with great danger at the door. It didn't have to be that way if they would only return to God. This was an extraordinary spectacle that the universe could behold, seeing that Judah was guilty and acknowledging that God was justified in the course He was about to take against them. Not to punish them; they were punishing themselves, but to wake them up so He would be able to continue to bless them and fulfill His promises.

Now Isaiah, under God's guidance, turned his attention to the religious ceremonies in which the people regularly participated. The people of Jerusalem and Judah were as sinful as the people of Sodom and Gomorrah, and yet they kept sacrificing at the temple of the Lord. Those things in the temple service that God had designed to remind them of the coming Messiah had now become meaningless rituals because of their sinful lives. In fact, God hated those rituals. He said, "Stop doing it! I've had more than enough burnt offerings. I don't take any pleasure in the blood of animals. I can't bear your 'holy' assemblies! My soul hates your festivals! Your incense is detestable to me! I will not listen to your many prayers while your hands are full of blood!"

The lesson Isaiah wanted to impress upon Israel was the importance of holiness. Holy living is active living. It is even more than giving up sins. Righteous living is the only way to avoid iniquity. The people of Jerusalem needed to offer, as well as experience, justice. The oppressed, the fatherless, and the widows all needed care and compassion. God is always on the side of the victims.

Isaiah, the Prophet

The oppressors must realize that they were arraying themselves against all the might and power of Heaven.

God invited them to discuss with Him what could be done about their situation. They should be aware of how bad the conditions were in their lives. He wanted to make everything right and do more for them than they could imagine. He intended to bring their city back to how it had been when it was a shining light to the nations around it. In fact, he would make it even better than that. The alternative was grim. It was their choice whether they would seek the good in harmony with God or whether they would receive the bad by rebelling against God and not allowing Him to work for them. They needed to know that those who forsake God are forsaking the fountain of living waters. In doing so, they seal their own doom.

Isaiah read to Yishka what he had written. She looked very solemn and said, "If that is what God directed you to write, then it is what you should deliver. How did you know to say that Jerusalem is like a hut in the middle of a field? It is not like that now."

"I just sensed that it was the right thing to say."

"My dear husband, I believe it is prophetic. We are beginning to see what God has planned for you. Time will tell, but I think you are a prophet!"

Then Isaiah knew exactly how Ruel had felt when he said there was no way God would put a prophetess in his home (Isa. 8:3). He looked at Yishka, then put his head in his hands and felt his heart sink. What could he say? He did not want any more responsibility.

Yishka put her arms around him and asked, "Where will your message go from here?"

Aware that that was an important question, he laid aside his feelings and answered, "I'm not exactly sure. Should I read it in the palace? Or should I read it in the temple? This will be the first time people hear something like this from me. What will they think?"

"Read it first to my father and his friends. See what they advise you."

"That's a very good idea. I will go there this afternoon. Will you go with me?"

"Yes, I'll be happy to go. I would like to watch their faces as they hear this."

Isaiah added, "I will not tell the others, but I will tell you that I also plan to read it to King Uzziah. He is receiving great blessings from reading the scrolls. He is actually memorizing them. He tells me he wishes he had taken time to study them before. It would have made all the difference. I want to see what he says about this message."

As could be expected, the reaction of godly people was positive. They appreciated the good news as well as understanding the reason for the bad news.

Ruel spoke for all of them when he expressed amazement. "Just imagine! God invites sinful people to come, to discuss with Him, to reason together" (Isa. 1:18). What kind of God must He be to suggest that? And He has such good plans for us, even when so much sin abounds around His holy city. We need to share these ideas everywhere. So many people think He is out to get us, that we have no chance of escaping punishment from Him. This makes me think it is someone else who is sending the punishment and then trying to blame it on God."

Isaiah spoke up, "So where would you suggest I go next with this message?"

"To the temple," said one. "To the palace" said others. "Both places," responded several.

"I believe you are right," Isaiah said. "And before Yishka and I leave, I would ask you to have prayer with us. Please pray that minds will be open to receive this message. Pray that I will have the courage and conviction to present it properly. Pray that Jerusalem will turn to God and become a holy city, filled with faithfulness to Him so He can do for us what He would like to be able to do."

Several prayed, and as the last man prayed, he added this phrase, "And thank you, our Father, that You have sent us a new prophet." And the whole group responded with a hearty "Amen."

Uzziah had much the same response. His love and appreciation for Isaiah were great. With tears in his eyes, he said, "God could not have found a better man. All your life He has been preparing you for this. May He bless and strengthen you to share His messages with the people who will not be happy to hear them."

Again, Isaiah's heart almost failed him when he thought of himself as a prophet. Only his faith in God's guiding could carry him through.

*****

The crowds at both the temple and the palace were happy to listen to a message from Isaiah. He had such stature and influence that he must be about to say something good and important to them. But after listening to him, they started to grumble. "Who does he think he is, to say we are as bad as Sodom and Gomorrah?"

"What's wrong with him? Doesn't he know we are God's special people, and He would never want anyone to talk to us like that!"

Isaiah, the Prophet

"At least nobody but one of the prophets. Some of them have had some harsh messages."

"And you know what happened to them! Isaiah better watch out."

"He must be under the influence of some legalistic people. I know who some of those could be."

"Maybe his father-in-law wrote that for him."

"No, I bet it was his wife. She 'gets messages,' you know. Ha ha, ha, ha, ha." They all laughed before they became serious again.

"I hope he does not come around with any more messages."

"And how would you stop Isaiah? He has more power and prestige in the court than anyone else."

"That's true. I guess I'll just leave if he comes to give another message."

That evening, when Isaiah reached home, he found to his surprise that Anyah was waiting for him. She did not look happy. Yishka had offered her some food which she had refused. She didn't want to talk to anyone but her son.

"How could you do this to me?" she fumed.

"Do what? What have I done to you?" Isaiah asked.

"Embarrassed me forever in front of my friends!"

"Okay, I guess you had better explain what you are talking about. Were you at the temple today when I spoke?"

"No, I was not. I was enjoying myself at the best high place. But it didn't take long to hear what a fool you had made of yourself!"

"Your evaluation does not match that of everyone who heard me."

"Oh yes, and what did they say?" she queried.

"That God must have given me the words of the message because they fit perfectly with what is happening in Jerusalem and throughout Judah."

"I was told that you said Jerusalem is no better than a hut."

"I did say that, and I'm not sure why I did, but those were the words that came to me. Maybe in a few years we will see that happen."

Anyah was exasperated. "Are you saying that you were prophesying?"

"We will have to wait and see. And what is it to you? Right now I have an appointment with a friend." With that, Isaiah stomped out of the house, ignoring supper and leaving his mother sitting there.

Yishka could understand his reaction, since she had heard many stories from him about his mother. Nevertheless, one's mother is to be respected, right? So, what was she supposed to do now to smooth over his disrespect? After a few uncomfortable minutes, she hesitantly invited Anyah to walk out in the garden with her. Not knowing what else to do, Anyah followed her daughter-in-law outside. Yishka talked about what she had started and what she hoped to do in the garden and asked Anyah if she had ever had a garden.

"No," she definitely had not. She had never thought of doing any gardening, because she lived in the palace and all of that was taken care of by gardeners.

Yishka asked, "How would you like to plant something here just to watch it grow and see how it works?"

If it had been anyone else, she probably would have abruptly refused. But Yishka was so gentle and sweet that Anyah suddenly thought, *"Why not?"*

"Yes," she said. "I would like to try it out. Would you like to have rosemary and parsley in your yard? They taste so good in food."

"Oh, yes, I would love to have them. I've been thinking that we needed to plant herbs so they would be right here and fresh when we want to use them."

"Okay," agreed Anyah. "I know where to get some plants and I'll bring them tomorrow." With that, she escaped without any more conversation.

The peace and quiet after the storm was a relief. Now Yishka waited for Isaiah to come back so she could tell him what had happened. When he finally dared come back home, he apologized for leaving her to pick up the pieces. He said he realized that his bad attitude toward his mother was something he needed to pray about.

* * * * *

Isaiah, the Prophet 49

Over the next few years, Isaiah felt the burden to speak to the nation four more times. (You can read those messages in the Old Testament's book of Isaiah, chapters 2, 3, 4, and 5.) Just as he did while writing court history, he thought long and hard about how to word the messages from God, first to make them memorable; then also to reflect the purest and best writing in Hebrew literature. As he wrote, it became more and more obvious that he was often predicting what would happen in the future. Often, the message about the future was God's exciting plans for a renewed kingdom of righteousness. Other times it was a warning about the future for those who rebelled against God—that their leadership was to be taken away; and there would be famine and misery. But then again, God would promise, "Tell the righteous it will be well with them, for they will enjoy the fruit of their deeds" (Isa. 3:10). But His words also made it clear that God was not arbitrarily causing anyone to suffer. "They have brought disaster upon themselves" (Isa. 3:9). God, the righteous Judge, was paying attention to what was happening and, in time, their futures would be settled with fairness and justice. Even the women were warned that they would suffer for their ungodly and shallow attitudes and actions. Again, though, the message would return to the glorious future God planned for the righteous. There would be survivors and the Branch of the Lord would provide everything they needed. Because of all their godless behavior, God was giving permission to the surrounding nations to come and almost destroy Judah.

Also, during King Uzziah's lifetime, there was a very strong earthquake. People had to flee for their lives (Zech.14:5). Some were crushed and killed by falling debris. Many interpreted that event as a call from God to come into harmony with Him if they wanted to continue living rather than to die in such a disaster. Archaeologists have found evidence in the area for an earthquake of that strength.

A great relief to Isaiah at this time was the news that Micah, a godly man from Moresheth, about twenty-five miles southwest of Jerusalem, was beginning to preach the same messages of warning to sinners, as well as God's love and compassion for His people.

Although there were those who complained, a growing segment of the population thought the messages were exactly what Judah and Jerusalem needed. Both Isaiah and Micah were referred to more and more often as prophets. King Jotham was supportive of their messages, but he still did not do anything to change the situation in the nation. Uzziah's health had progressively declined. He still memorized the scrolls, and Isaiah still visited him, reading him his messages. It seemed that his death could happen soon.

The most surprising development during those years was that Anyah loved gardening. She planted herbs and then more herbs and then more yet. Hardly a day went by that she wasn't in the yard nurturing her plants. Yishka treated her with respect and kindness. Anyah soon gave up trying to control her and grew to love her instead. Less surprising, Yishka and Isaiah had a baby daughter. How precious and loved she was. When the new baby arrived, Anyah instantly became an enthusiastic grandmother. She was in their house almost constantly. Isaiah was a bit offended that she had wanted nothing to do with him, but now she wanted everything to do with little Ruth. He was leery of the possible results and warned Yishka to never leave Anyah and the baby alone. He didn't want to come home some day and learn that his daughter had been taken to worship idols. Anyah was so occupied with the baby that she had little time for her usual complaints to Isaiah. He wasn't even sure she had time to go to worship the idols or visit the high places.

It was no surprise when word came that Uzziah's life was nearing its end. Isaiah was called because there were those who knew that he had continued visiting the leper even though he had limited physical contact with him. Hurrying to the little house in the back garden, he prayed with his cousin, his friend, and reassured him that a better life was soon to come for him. No one else came to visit or mourn. He died with Isaiah by his side. He could not be buried with the rest of Judah's kings because of his leprosy, but he was buried nearby in a field that was owned by the kings.

With one less responsibility, Isaiah dedicated himself more than ever to his family and his work. Under King Jotham, his court responsibilities were greater; he was now the chief historiographer for the kingdom. He had no intention of ignoring his wife and daughter. His happiest hours were with them. It seemed to him that he had written the messages that needed to be given. His responsibility for that was over. He would not have to be an on-going prophet. The idea was a huge relief. He would not have to continue to counter the resistance he had already experienced and that he knew would continue if he delivered more messages. He had done enough. He shrank from the thought of continuing to deliver messages of warning and reproof from God. The task seemed hopeless. It was Micah's turn to experience that rejection. Isaiah would go to the temple to pray about his decision. He felt sure God would understand.

Chapter Four:
Isaiah Sees God[12]

It was still the same year in which Uzziah had died. Isaiah expected a calm and peaceful life from now on. As he had intended, he went to the temple to pray. At that time, the Hebrew word for *temple* designated it as the "palace" of the great King of heaven. Standing in the court of the men, facing west with the veil over the Holy Place before him, his thoughts wandered to the day he had come for King Uzziah. But that was not what he was here for! His recent thoughts about why he should not continue to do the work of a prophet crowded his mind. He began to pray earnestly that God would listen to his prayer. Even though he did not want to be a prophet, he surely wanted God to control his life.

Suddenly the view before him changed. Instead of the building in front of him, he saw into the Most Holy Place! There he saw God's throne high and lifted up. And on the throne sat God wearing a robe that reached all the way down, over, and through the temple. Above Him, on each side, were angels with six wings, calling out to each other, "Holy, holy, holy is the Lord Almighty. The whole earth is full of His glory." At the sound of their voices, the building shook and the temple filled with smoke.

Isaiah fell to his knees. His life passed before him in a moment, and he saw how sinful and unclean he was. At the same time, he glimpsed the loveliness of God's character. Before this, he had felt pretty good about his spirituality and

---

12   This chapter is largely drawn from Isaiah, chapter 6 and the book *Prophets and Kings*, chapter 25, "The Call of Isaiah."

his values. Now, in comparison, he perceived the righteousness of God and realized he was nothing, and probably about to die, because no one could see God and live.

Isaiah cried, "Woe is me!" …. "I am ruined! For I am a man of unclean lips, and I live among a people of unclean lips, and my eyes have seen the King, the Lord Almighty." In the last message Isaiah had written, he had pronounced six woes upon the sinners among God's people (Isa. 5:8–24). Now, profoundly aware of his own imperfection of character, he pronounced this seventh woe against himself.

As he knelt in terror and anticipation of death, one of the angels flew to him with a live coal which he had taken with tongs from the altar of incense. Helping Isaiah to stand up, he touched his mouth and said, "See, this has touched your lips; your guilt is taken away and your sin atoned for." A most wonderful sense of freedom replaced the fear Isaiah had felt. He would never be the same again. The realization of the glory and holiness of God led him to stand in true humility before Him.

Isaiah Sees God

Then he heard the voice of the Lord saying, "Whom shall I send? And who will go for us?"

Totally forgetting his intention to explain to God that he didn't want to be a prophet, Isaiah heard himself say with total truthfulness, "Here am I. Send me!" The honor and privilege of serving with God was far beyond anything he could imagine for himself. And now God gave him a forewarning of what to expect: the people would not accept what he was to tell them.

How could anyone reject a message from God? He could not understand that, so he asked, "How long will this continue?"

The answer was disheartening. "Until the cities and houses and fields are ruined. Until I have sent everyone into captivity and the land is utterly forsaken." Fortunately, the end of the story was a little bit better. The Lord would preserve the land, and a tenth part of the people.

For a long time, the spirit of evil had worked on leading people to think that God was the author of sin and suffering and death. They imagined Him to be hard and exacting, watching for any chance to denounce and condemn them. Most had become wrapped in "…a veil of ignorance…. Error and superstition flourished."[13] The truth is that God pities every person, because we are all captive victims in this sinful world. We cannot possibly save ourselves. Isaiah became the prophet of hope, teaching that God is the great Healer of spiritual disease.

At the time he could not know it, but his work was not to be in vain. Some gave earnest heed and turned from their idols to the worship and knowledge of Jehovah. Over time, his words were to continue bearing fruit in decided reformation. His message was to be so eternal in its application that his book would continue to the end of time to instruct and encourage. You and I today are reading his book still, showing how Isaiah belongs to the ages, not just to the people of his time.

Despite the sadness he felt over the rejection of God by His own people, Isaiah reveled in the fact that God had spoken to him, his sins had been removed, he had willingly agreed to be a prophet, and nothing would ever change that. His task in life would be to bear God's message of warning and hope, so God's people might catch a vision of the love and holiness of God and be saved as a result.

As he left the temple, it struck him that his experience had similarities with King Uzziah's sin in the temple. Both had to do with the golden altar in the Holy Place, and with coals from the altar. King Uzziah went there with a rebel-

---

13   Ellen G. White, *Prophets and Kings* (Mountain View, CA: Pacific Press Publishing Association, 1943), 371.1.

lious spirit to do something that was totally forbidden by God. The results were ominous, but God used that event to bring Uzziah into a deeper relationship with Himself. On the other hand, Isaiah went to the temple to pray about God's plan for his life. When God's intentions differed from his, Isaiah wholeheartedly accepted God's will without complaint. He sincerely agreed to do what God asked, knowing that it would only be accomplished by God's direction and help. He was humbled as well as astonished and excited by what had happened.

He hurried home, eager to tell Yishka. "Now we know what the message meant!"

Wanting to share his excitement, she asked, "What? What happened? What did you learn?"

Isaiah described what had happened. God had officially called him to be a prophet! Then he told her what God's message to him had been. Both of them were solemn as they talked about it.

Yishka asked, "Do you think God is making people reject His word?"

"I've wondered about that. But no, I don't think he is causing people to rebel. There is no evidence that He is that kind of a God. I think there is a different explanation. God knows what people are going to do, and He realizes that the vast majority are not going to change their way of life and their reaction to Him. So, He has just graciously let me know what I will be dealing with—what we will be dealing with—and what He plans to do about it. How good He is to have given you to me for a wife. You truly are my helper. Think how discouraging this work would be if He had not warned me of the results."

"But we know a lot of people who are faithful to God. What about them? Will they have to suffer because of the evil people?" asked Yishka.

Isaiah thought deeply, then he spoke. "In the scrolls are many stories about good people who suffered because of bad people. First there was Adam and Eve and Abel, then the flood came because of the vast majority who were not faithful to God. But there must have been some good people whose families didn't let them get on the ark. The earth was filled with violence. God could not let that continue to jeopardize his plans to send a Messiah. Who else can you think of?"

"Joseph," suggested Yishka.

"Yes, of course that's right. And don't forget that Jacob suffered terribly during the many years that followed before He found out that Joseph was alive in Egypt. Remember also how Moses had to put up with so much rebellion on the way to the Promised Land."

Yishka continued, "Then, during the time of the judges, there must have been some faithful people who had to endure the trials that came because of those who forgot God."

"I'm sure there were. And we could come up with other examples. God is guiding and He does what He thinks is best. He is not the one who is causing the trouble. When we are on God's side, it doesn't matter so much if we have to suffer trials caused by evil, because God will take care of us and make it right for us in the end."

That conversation had helped Isaiah think through the ideas that initially perplexed him. Day and night, he thought about the wonderful experience of seeing God. He was changed forever. Never would he forget what God had done for him. Up to now, he had been a righteous man. From now on, he was God's man, constantly aware of God's desire to be with His people. His closeness to God would grow and grow to the end of his life. When perils encompassed God's people and the powers of darkness seemed about to prevail, he would direct their minds to look upward toward God on His throne, where He directed the affairs of heaven and earth.

Yishka had a slightly different reaction. While she was thrilled to know God's plans for Isaiah, she was perplexed about God's plans for her. Since the message she had received for Isaiah before their engagement, she had not received any other message from God. Her life until then had been defined by the fact that she received messages. Was that never to happen again? Now that she was married, did that mean that God had no more use for her to warn or encourage other people?

One day she tried to express this perplexity to Isaiah, but he didn't seem to understand. Wasn't she happy with her life with him? What difference did it make? He was consumed by his career, and also now by his writing and preaching, so it was difficult for him to take time to empathize with her questioning. She gave up trying to explain, but she continued to think and pray about her situation. She felt she needed to see God's guiding in her life as well as in her husband's. Ultimately, she clung to the memory of the last instruction when God had said she would be Isaiah's helper. That was what she would do her best to be until further directions came.

King Jotham would be on the throne for another seven years after Uzziah died. He was successful in some construction work in Jerusalem and other places around the area, mostly building up defenses against encroaching enemies. He waged war against the Ammonites who were east of the Jordan River, and he won. They paid tribute to him for at least three years. He stayed loyal to God but didn't do much of anything to help his people change their godless ways (2 Chron. 27:1–6). King Jotham's son, Ahaz, who had married at an early age, had a growing family of several children. Isaiah was familiar with them and felt that Ahaz was a bully, and maybe even worse. He feared what would happen when Ahaz came to the throne, but for now he had many other things to think about.

It was during King Jotham's reign that God laid the burden of prophesying on Micah. He was a prophet to the countryside, while Isaiah witnessed for God in the palace and the city of Jerusalem. The messages were similar, and sometimes were almost identical. Each one was blessed by the example of the other.

During those years, Isaiah and Yishka had another daughter and then a son. He was very special, because God gave him his name, Shear-Jashub, meaning "A remnant will return" (Isa. 7:3).

King Uzziah had been the chief obstacle to Tiglath-Pileser, the king of Assyria, who was conquering Western Asia. With Uzziah gone, it seemed to be only a question of time before Judah would be overwhelmed and Assyria would control the known world. Assyria was making yearly raids on the surrounding countries and, without doubt, Judah would be targeted soon. Meanwhile, there was bad blood with Israel to the north where King Amaziah had lost a war (2 Kings 14:9). There was no love lost with the city of Sela in the land of Edom southeast of the Dead Sea which had been captured by Amaziah. The Arameans (Syria) to the northeast with Damascus as their capital were preparing to create conflict with Judah. In other words, Judah was surrounded by enemies. Without a heartfelt return to God, they were keeping themselves away from His protection. They made it impossible for Him to give all the help and blessings He wanted them to have.

God was leading Isaiah to recognize that He was not only concerned for Judah, plus Israel. God's love reaches everywhere. Salvation is available to everyone.

As Judah became more and more involved with the surrounding world, God was leading Isaiah to recognize that He was not only concerned for Judah, plus Israel. God's love reaches everywhere. Salvation is available to everyone. It is based on personal choice, not national identify. Salvation became the heart of Isaiah's message.

PART III:

Ahaz, the King[14]

---
14 The stories of Ahaz are largely drawn from 2 Kings 16; 2 Chronicles, chapter 28; and Isaiah, chapter 7.

Chapter Five:
The Gloom of Night Approaches

Indeed, Isaiah had been right. He was a bully. As soon as Ahaz began to rule on his own, people noticed the difference between the soft style of King Jotham's reign and the harshness now being seen everywhere. Nobody could explain the situation better than his own children. The oldest daughter was ironically named Athaliah, which means "God is exalted." He wanted to sacrifice her to the god Moloch, but her mother prevailed to save her since she was a girl. His second daughter he did sacrifice. Athaliah, as young as she was, knew to stay far away from him. His first son was also sacrificed. At least two sons lived long enough to grow up, and one of them was heard to say, "My daddy is mean and wanted to sacrifice me, but my grandfather told me to pray to God, and He saved me." That child's name was Hezekiah (2 Kings 1:20).

King Jotham had apparently had a good influence on his grandson, but none on his son. Ahaz had an idolatrous mother, perhaps from the northern kingdom of Israel. From an early age, she taught him to side with those who rejected God. They said the God of heaven had not answered their prayers, so they would follow other gods who paid more attention to them. They did not believe in God's promises, because they complained that they never came true. When they prayed to Baal or to Moloch, they made money gambling. God never helped them with that. When they worshiped at the high places, they had fun and experienced captivating sensual experiences. That never happened at

The Gloom of Night Approaches

the temple. Besides, they sometimes saw priests from the temple taking part in the idol worship at the high places.

Those with total resistance to God and His worship reinterpreted the history of Judah and Israel. They thought Ahab and Jezebel and their family had been martyrs. The hundreds of priests of Baal who had been slaughtered had been martyrs (1 Kings 18:18-19). Queen Athaliah was remembered as a martyr (2 Kings 11:1-3; 14-16). Those who opposed them were the wicked ones. It was the God of Judah who caused their deaths. Those who rebelled against God thought there was nothing special about being descended from King David because, they reasoned, no Messiah would ever come. Whoever was the strongest seized the power. Right now, it was Ahaz. He intended to remain king for a very long time. He would do what the gods told him to do so that they would help him.

Obviously, his first daughter's name came from this kind of twisted thinking. She was an exceptional child from the first. By the time she was seven, Athaliah had watched what happened to little girls when they were married, and she determined she would not get married. After some time to think about how she could avoid it, she hit upon the perfect plan. First, she had to be brave enough to talk to her father. Her mother would never approve of her idea, as it could expose her to danger. Watching for an opportunity when he was not in a terrible mood, she approached him.

"Father, I know that you wanted to give me to the god Moloch."

He nodded, wondering what in the world she was talking about. He almost never saw her or spoke a word to her. She was just a useless girl in his mind.

"Since you did not get to give me to him, would it be okay for me to go and be his priestess?"

He was touched that she had thought of this and would want to fulfill her father's wishes. Besides, he needed to do something special for Moloch in order to get on better terms with him, or at least on better terms with his priests.

"Dear child, do you really want to do this? It means you would not get married and have your own family." What he was really thinking was how helpful it would be to avoid coming up with a dowry for her. She could be a useful political tool for him.

"Yes, Father, I really want to do this."

"Then you shall. We will not tell your mother until all the arrangements have been made."

It only took a few days for her to become an unbeliever. From watching the other priestesses and listening to the conversation of the priests, she realized that what went on here was hocus pocus.

In this matter, he was as good as his word. By the time she was ten years old, Athaliah was dressed in sparkling white robes and serving as a priestess to the god Moloch. In order to escape having an undesirable husband, she fixed her heart on serving this powerful god, believing what she had been told about him. It only took a few days for her to become an unbeliever. From watching the other priestesses and listening to the conversation of the priests, she realized

The Gloom of Night Approaches

that what went on here was hocus pocus. This was no powerful god. Powerful priests, yes, some events were hard to explain, but nothing else, nothing that she could believe in. So now what was she to do?

From that moment on she didn't believe in what she was doing, but she was royalty, and she did her work well, so she was promoted often. By the time she was in her early twenties, she was the high priestess. Highly intelligent, she never told anyone what she really thought. She became so popular with those who came to worship, that they gave her a special name. She was always referred to as "The Virgin."

* * * * *

Meanwhile, other events were afoot in Judah. Because of King Ahaz' total involvement in idolatry, God allowed the Arameans from the kingdom to the northeast to defeat him and take many prisoners to their capital, Damascus. As soon as that tragedy passed, God gave Ahaz into the hands of the king of Israel who inflicted heavy casualties. In one day, King Pekah of Israel killed one hundred and twenty thousand soldiers in Judah. Zicri, an Ephraimite soldier, killed Ahaz' son Maaseiah, as well as the officer in charge of the palace, and the man who was second to the king (2 Chron. 6–8). When Isaiah realized what had happened right in the palace, not far from where he worked, he thought surely this would bring King Ahaz to his senses. But worse events lay ahead. Rampaging through the streets of Jerusalem and other nearby towns, the victorious Israelite soldiers herded together two hundred thousand women and children and began marching them out of the city. Girls who struggled were violated in the process. One little girl, not old enough to marry, was raped when she tried to hide inside the temple precincts. Wailing and moaning, she was dragged into the line. There she hunched over, clutching her torn clothing, weeping inconsolably. Two beautifully dressed women came over to her. One of them shook her shoulder gently and spoke.

"You are one of us now. We recognize the symptoms. We all cried like that at first. You have to face the fact that your life will never be the same again. 'Once impure, always impure.' That's what people think. Stay with us. We'll do all we can to take care of you." They wanted to stay with her, but soldiers grabbed them and shoved them into a different part of the line.

The desolate little girl could hardly take in what they were talking about. Whatever it was, it did not sound good to her. And their kindness didn't make her feel any better.

Many of the group were not dressed warmly enough for evening or night temperatures. That didn't bother their captors at all. They were plundering every house and shop and then piling their loot on the backs of the poor captives.

In the midst of this melee, a motherly looking woman with a small child in hand appeared. A few minutes before, she had been calmly going about her afternoon chores. Suddenly it came. Faintly at first, then stronger. With a start, she recognized it from long before. "Come, my child," she said. "We have someone to encourage."

"What's encourage?" asked the child.

"You'll see," replied her kindly mother.

As they walked through town, they saw that something bad was going on. People were running and crying. There were many soldiers and clouds of dust from flying horses' hooves. Yishka picked up her second daughter, Naomi, and held her close as they continued through the crowds. At last they came to a long, ragged line of people being closely guarded by soldiers. They could hear a lot of yelling and cursing.

"Those men are talking bad," said Naomi.

"Yes, they are," responded Yishka. "But don't be afraid. God will protect us." She was looking carefully at the people in line. She would know who it was when the time came. They walked a long way down the line of captives. Finally, Yishka knew who she was looking for. A young girl, not many years older than Naomi was wailing hopelessly in the line.

Yishka walked over, set Naomi down, and hugged the little girl. "You will finally have a home and family," she said.

Shocked, the child stopped crying and looked up. She did not know the woman who had hugged her. "Who are you?" she asked.

"I'm known as the prophetess. God sent me to encourage you."

The girl was stunned into silence. Could she believe what she was hearing? Was it possible the Great God had sent someone to help her? She knew about prophets, but she had never heard of a prophetess.

A soldier was coming toward them. "Quickly. Tell me your mother's name and where she lives. I will go and give her a message as well."

The girl barely had time to give the name and address before the soldier brutally pulled Yishka and Naomi away from the line of captives. He had already looked her over and decided her child was too young, and there was something about her he did not want to tangle with. "Get away from here right now," he commanded.

Yishka calmly picked up Naomi and walked away. "Mommy, did he hurt you?"

"No. I am fine. God protected us. We need to pray for all these sad people."

"Should we pray for the bad ones, too?"

"Yes, we should pray for them as well, that they will learn to worship God."

She continued, "Now we are going to look for the little girl's mother. She will be worried about what happened to her child." Fortunately, the mother was at home, and Yishka was able to explain what had happened, leaving out the details, and reassuring the mother that God would protect her daughter and bring her home again.

Yishka pondered how God could possibly bring back the little girl, but God did not reveal that to her. Saddened by what she had seen, but secretly thrilled that God had chosen to use her again, she waited for Isaiah to come home and tell her more about the events of the day. It was with great relief that he found her and their daughters and little son when he reached home. Later in the evening, Anyah appeared. She had spent much of the day in hiding. Now that the soldiers and the captives had left town, she also wanted to come and see if everyone was safe in Isaiah's home. When she saw all of them, she said, "Thank God!"

Isaiah and Yishka looked at each other with shock. Had they heard correctly? Neither one of them said anything, but they hoped the phrase was more than a passing thought in an emergency. The family ate supper in a somber mood, thinking of all the families that had lost their sons and fathers; also, the families torn apart by the women and children taken captive. When Anyah looked as if she was going to leave, Yishka invited her to stay with them and she accepted with alacrity.

* * * * *

The captives, stunned by what had happened to them and staggering as they were forced to continue marching through the evening and into the night, stumbled down the steep and rocky road toward the Jordan River. Those old enough to think about it, tried not to imagine what their future would be as slaves to the Israelites. Women with their children struggled to stay together. Smaller children were picked up and carried so they would not lag behind and get lost. Some women without children found those who were alone and tried to help and comfort them. The little girl named Tabitha who had received the message was determined to avoid the fancy women who had approached her.

Instead, she was able to attach herself to a sympathetic woman who reminded her of her mother. Finally, when they had almost reached the river, the mass of people was allowed to stop for the night. With no food and no bedding, it was a miserable night. They were able to drink some water from a creek near their makeshift camp. Those without adequate clothes huddled together, trying to stay warm. They had covered almost twenty miles. Even though they were used to walking almost everywhere they went, most of the children had never walked so far.

Early morning came at last with no prospects of anything better than the day before. Their muscles were stiff and sore. They needed more sleep, and they certainly needed food. But there was none. They saw the soldiers eating, but not a bite was brought to them. The women looked for any fruit trees or wild herbs that might assuage their children's hunger, but little was found.

Soon they were forced to begin marching again. Once they reached the Jordan River, at least the road beside it was smoother and mostly level. That made their journey a little bit easier. On the other hand, the weather was hotter. Those who had been cold the night before, rejoiced until they got so hot that they yearned for the cool of the coming night. Tabitha hung on to the thought that God had said she had a future. What kind, she did not know, but at least she was not going to die on this march. It was a long, hard day. They marched more than twenty miles. That night they camped by a river that flowed into the Jordan. Its water was cleaner, so they had enough to drink. Those who knew something about this area realized that the next day would be about another twenty-mile march, bringing them to the city of Samaria. Then their dreaded fate would be decided. Marching while hungry was almost better than that.

That night and the next morning were a repeat of the night and day before. How could they possibly go another day without food? But they had to keep marching. Women carried the little children. Now they began to see more people as they passed the smaller towns near Samaria. Those they saw looked wonderingly at them. The soldiers were proud of what they had done and were happy to tell the passersby that they could come to the city of Samaria and get their pick of slaves.

Mid-afternoon, as they approached the large city, two men came toward them on donkeys. It was soon obvious that they had already heard what had happened and intended to talk to the first soldiers they encountered. The older man introduced himself as the prophet Oded.

Without polite preamble, he started in on the soldiers, "Because the LORD, the God of your ancestors, was angry with Judah, he gave them into your hand.

The Gloom of Night Approaches

But you have slaughtered them in a rage that reaches to heaven. And now you intend to make these women and children of Judah and Jerusalem your slaves.

"Aren't you also guilty of sins against the Lord your God? Now listen to me! Send back your fellow countrymen you have taken as prisoners, for the Lord's fierce anger rests on you."

One of the soldiers responded harshly. "Be still, old man! We don't have to listen to you. This is what war is all about! We haven't done anything wrong, and we deserve to have something for our trouble." Looking around, he noticed that some of the other soldiers were looking sheepish. He was just about to order them to fall into line when another larger group approached.

The captives who were near enough to hear were paying close attention as they waited to see what would happen.

This time it was the major leaders from the tribe of Ephraim, four prominent men. Some of the soldiers recognized them and realized that they had to be respectful. These men had no time or patience for young arrogant soldiers.

"You must not bring those prisoners here," the spokesman said, "or we will be guilty before the LORD. Do you intend to add to our sin and guilt? For our guilt is already great, and His fierce anger rests on Israel."

Several soldiers gathered to discuss what had just happened. First, the prophet had told them this was their sin and God was angry with them. Now the leadership was claiming that all Israel would bear the blame. They were a nation mostly of idolaters; Assyria was closing in on them. They couldn't afford to add to their guilt.

Those with the coolest heads among the soldiers hastened to agree with the prominent men. Then the highest-ranking soldiers agreed. Finally, even the common soldiers thought about the chance that they might have to fight the Assyrian army. With that, all the soldiers walked away with just their own belongings. The captives were left alone with the plunder and the four prominent men.

A group of mothers hesitantly walked over to the men who were discussing what to do. "Please sirs, our children have had nothing to eat for three days."

The men were appalled. "You walked all this way, and the soldiers did not feed you anything?"

"No, sir."

A crowd, curious to see who this massive group of people was, had gathered around by this time. The spokesman called out to them. "Go into the city and get every loaf of bread and bring milk for the children. Bring whatever other food you can find that is ready to eat. These poor people are starving."

Many of the captives began to cry. They were so relieved after their horrendous trip that the thought of food and perhaps freedom was overwhelming.

> *Go into the city and get every loaf of bread and bring milk for the children. Bring whatever other food you can find that is ready to eat. These poor people are starving.*

Next, the leaders appointed some of the crowd to help go through the plunder and find clothes and sandals for those who obviously needed them. A call went out for donkeys that the young and the weak could ride. Tabitha received sandals and a full set of clothes to replace those she had been trying to hold around her during the three-day march. Food arrived in abundance. It seemed that everyone was eager to help. All of the captives ate and drank to the full. They were going back home! They were speechless with amazement.

Before the group could head home, they needed to spend the night. Families took in mothers with their children. The size of the group overwhelmed the city's capacity, so others brought blankets and mats that could be used for camping outside. Guards were posted to protect them during the night. Everything possible was done to make them comfortable. They couldn't believe their change of fortune.

In the morning, some of the mothers were asked to advise the leadership of Samaria on whether they felt the trip home should begin that day or whether they needed to rest longer. Every one of them wanted to start back immediately. The thought of their families waiting an extra day to know what had happened to them was unthinkable. All of the plunder was loaded on donkeys. Other donkeys carried children and any adult who felt too weak to walk. Yet more donkeys carried loads of food and drink and camping supplies for the trip.

The group of four men decided to accompany them to be sure they were safe on the way. The trip south was totally different from the trip north. There was almost a holiday mood among them. If faster travelers passed them, they were asked to spread the word that the women and children were on their way home and should be met at Jericho with food and blankets and donkeys for overnight and the trip back up the mountains to Jerusalem or other nearby towns where they had been captured. It was only necessary to spend one night with the guards on the way back. The last night and day would be with their friends and families camping near Jericho.

The Gloom of Night Approaches

After they set up camp, the guards spent the evening organizing the groups that would go to each town. That way, those who were not met in Jericho by family would have protection and companionship on their way home.

The word spread quickly that the captives were returning. It was almost unbelievably good news. Yishka heard and prayed a prayer of thanksgiving for Tabitha and all the others. A huge crowd traveled down to Jericho to meet the captives and accompany them home. They were aware that many of them would discover that members of their family had been killed in the battle. They would need support of various kinds as they dealt with their loss. But first they would all need to spend the night before returning.

Isaiah accompanied the group to Jericho and preached to the huge assembly, leading them in praising God for His goodness in saving their lives and overturning their captivity. They thanked God for the many Israelites who had sacrificed to make them comfortable and get them home safely. They expressed gratitude that almost all of the plunder would be returned to its owners. Then they prayed for the families of the dead soldiers who would now have to cope without their loved ones. Many of them would not know the fate of their family members until they returned to the towns where they lived. Finally, Isaiah pleaded with the group to turn wholeheartedly to God and worship Him only. Then He would be able to provide all the safety and blessings He wanted to give them. In light of what had happened that week, with so many killed, and so many captured but then returned, the mood in the crowd was one of heartfelt desire to live in harmony with God.

The guards who had accompanied them from Samaria slipped away as soon as they saw that their charges would be cared for. Lines of donkeys went back with them to their owners. For hours they traveled that night, wanting to put as much distance as possible between themselves and the groups from Judah. They were not sure whether or not some of the men would want to take vengeance on them for what the army had done. As they talked along the way, they discussed why it was that God had protected the women and children from captivity. Idolatry was so widespread in the northern kingdom of Israel, that it was hardly necessary to talk about it. But the southern kingdom of Judah had claimed to remain faithful to God. The guards wondered whether their gods would protect them from the Assyrians. It would not be long before they would find out.

* * * * *

Soon afterwards, Rezin, the king of Aram (Syria), and Pekah, the king of Israel, joined together to defeat King Ahaz, put in a king of their own choosing, and then force Judah to join them in their fight against the Assyrians (2 Kings 15:37). The first time they came, Judah suffered a disastrous defeat, but Jerusalem was not taken. The enemies did not succeed, because God was determined to keep a descendant of David on the throne of Judah. But they did capture Elath, a town at the north end of the Gulf of Aqaba and chased out all the people of Judah who lived there. When they left, Edomites, the descendants of Esau, moved in and have kept the town to this day.

But they weren't finished trying to capture Jerusalem. They managed to get the Ephraimites to unite with them. When King Ahaz and his associates heard that all three groups were coming to do battle with them, their hearts "…were shaken, as the trees of the forest are shaken by the wind." Ahaz was terror stricken at the prospect of being driven from the throne. An apostate, he had no intention of trusting God even though it appeared to him that his kingdom was soon to fall.

"Then the Lord said to Isaiah, 'Go out, you and your son Shear-Jashub [A Remnant Shall Return] to meet Ahaz at the end of the aqueduct of the Upper Pool, on the road to the Launderer's Field. Say to him, 'Be careful, keep calm and don't be afraid. Do not lose heart because of these two smoldering stubs of firewood.'" One more flicker and they will be gone. Their plan was directed against God and could not succeed.

God sent Isaiah to the place where Hezekiah would later start his famous tunnel that brought water into the city. At the time of King Ahaz, this source of water was outside the city. Undoubtedly some steps were already being contemplated as to how the water might be brought into the city and denied to an enemy outside the walls.

Isaiah continued with the words God had given him., Rezin of Aram (Syria), and Ephraim and Pekah of Israel "…have plotted your ruin, saying, 'Let us invade Judah; let us tear it apart and divide it among ourselves, and make that Syrian Tabeel (whose name means "good is god") king over it.'"

"But this is what the sovereign Lord says, 'It will not take place. It will not happen. If you do not stand firm in your faith, you will not stand at all.'"

Continuing, Isaiah gave King Ahaz the words from God: "Ask the Lord for a sign. It is your choice whether it be in the depths of the sea or high up in the sky."

But King Ahaz said, "I will not ask, I will not put the LORD to the test. I don't believe in Him and will not bother to ask for a sign." Ahaz refused to be persuaded. He did not want to believe, and he wanted nothing that might help

The Gloom of Night Approaches

him believe. The help he sought was that of Assyria, not of God. However, he was to have a sign in spite of himself. For the encouragement of those who would remain faithful in the years of crisis ahead, God saw fit to provide assurance that He would be with them.

Nobody but Isaiah, an esteemed member of the royal family, could get by with talking to the king this way. He continued, "Listen to me, you house of David! Is it not enough for you to try the patience of men? Will you also try the patience of my God?"

"For that reason, the Lord himself will give you a sign: A mature young woman will be with child and will give birth to a son and will call him Immanuel ("God with us"). When he is twelve years old, he will eat well on curds and honey." Curded milk (yogurt) was considered a delicacy and that, together with honey, implied an abundance of food. "But when he is very young, before he is old enough to know the difference between right and wrong, the land of the two kings you dread will be laid waste. Then the Lord will bring on you the Assyrians, a kingdom far worse than the two you fear."

The Immanuel sign would testify to God's presence with His people to guide, to protect, and to bless. "Many Old Testament prophecies have a twofold application such as this, first to the more immediate future and then to the more remote future"[15] and the eventual coming of the Messiah. And both applications of this prophecy came to pass! When Immanuel was two or three, Damascus fell to Assyria. When He was twelve, Samaria fell to Assyria. The few who were not then carried captive would find plenty to eat in the desolated land. There was still more to the message God had sent to King Ahaz: Isaiah said that the Lord will send "flies and bees" [Egypt and Assyria]. They will come and decimate the land so that briers and thorns take the place of vineyards and fertile fields. The few people who will be left will carry bows and arrows either as protection or to hunt. There will be plenty of good food for them to eat.

King Ahaz evidenced his scorn for everything Isaiah had told him. "I don't believe any of that for a minute!" he said. "Stop wasting my time and let me rule this country as I want to. You stick with your history writing and be sure you get it right!"

During King Ahaz' reign, Isaiah was frequently getting memos about not including certain events in the records. After all, Assyrian historians did not report the bad things that happened to their kings. Why should Isaiah leave a record of the few bad things that had happened to Ahaz? As a result, Isaiah

---

15   *Seventh-day Adventist Bible Commentary, Volume 4: Isaiah to Malachi* (Washington, DC: Review and Herald Publishing Association, 1955), p. 135.

followed a policy of keeping a second set of accurate records in his house. He could replace the official records after Ahaz was gone.

Assyrian sources indicate that King Uzziah had taken a strong stand against Assyria, and probably also his son Jotham had, but King Ahaz was friendly to Assyria. He sent gold and silver from the temple and from his own palace to Tiglath Pileser, the king of Assyria, in order to purchase Assyrian aid. It was the growing power of Assyria, not the waning kingdoms of Syria or Israel that Ahaz needed to worry about. During the next forty to fifty years, Judah would be all but swallowed up by Assyria, and King Ahaz was pursuing a policy that would inevitably play into Assyrian hands.

* * * * *

Athaliah had now put in years of pretending to follow something she did not believe in. She had status and influence and riches, and no husband, but sometimes she thought it was not enough. There must be more than she had. And then Jared walked into her life. He was a slave, forced to work in the temple of the gods. It didn't take her long to discover that he was a God worshiper, not an idolater. His father had been killed in the war with King Pekah, and the family land had been confiscated by the Philistines, so his mother had no choice but to give him up so that the rest of the family could survive. He was glad he could help his family, so he was never heard to complain about being a slave. "The Virgin" acted very distant and avoided him whenever anyone else was around, but when opportunities presented themselves, she and Jared found that they loved to talk. It always had to be done with great care. But he was such a dependable worker that he was soon assigned to clean up after closing time and prepare everything for the next morning. Since she was the high priestess; she lived there. That provided the time they yearned for, time to be together. It wasn't long before they both knew they were in love. Athaliah was fascinated with a feeling that she had never expected to experience.

Jared was evangelistic as well as loving. He wanted her to know how much peace and freedom she could have if she lived in harmony with the Great God. She laughed at him and said that all gods were fakes. She felt that if you believed, it was just in your mind. He responded that he hoped to live long enough to see her happy in the Lord.

With frequent opportunities and no witnesses, their relationship eventually turned physical. She had made it clear that she would never marry and intended to keep her job as long as she lived. Without any hope of an eventual

The Gloom of Night Approaches

life together, Jared finally ignored his beliefs, overcame his scruples, and started an affair with her. It was the most excitement both of them had ever had in their lives. Probably it was inevitable that the end came sooner than they could have guessed.

The chief priests of Moloch and Baal had a running and bitter competition to see which one could have more influence in the palace and which one could make more money from their worshipers. Jared was the slave of the chief priest of Moloch. He frequently went with his master to the palace for some assignment or other. A few months after he and Athaliah met, he was once again in the palace with the high priest. Both high priests with their slaves were there, arguing over their latest conflict. Tempers were flaring; voices were raised. Jared tried to tone down the fracas, which was becoming evident to every person within earshot and was embarrassing for both sides. The slave of the high priest of Baal who was behind Jared, drew a knife and sliced him down the back. He died almost immediately. He was only a slave, so his body was quickly removed and dumped into the trash that continually burned. Three days passed before Athaliah overheard what had happened to him. She was devastated but could not show it under any circumstances.

Life that had seemed normal before, now became unbearable. Then, within a month, she knew she was pregnant. It thrilled her that she was carrying Jared's child. But it gave her only a few months before people would find out and then she would be killed, stoned probably. Not only was she not married, but worse, she was "The Virgin" priestess. The punishment for breaking that vow was worse than the one for a pregnant and unmarried girl. Fortunately, her flowing white robes protected her for several months. That gave her time to decide what to do. One long night it came to her: she would declare that this baby was the child of a god. There were stories of such things happening. She hoped it would be a boy. A girl would be more difficult to pass off as sired by a god.

> *She would declare that this baby was the child of a god. There were stories of such things happening. She hoped it would be a boy. A girl would be more difficult to pass off as sired by a god.*

At eight months, she could wait no longer. She called together the high priest, and the other priests and priestesses. With great ceremony she informed them that the child she would soon have would be a demigod. She had been infused by one of the gods who especially wanted to bestow favor on their country by sending this child. She didn't announce it earlier because she could hardly herself believe the honor that was being bestowed on all of them. She had waited to be sure it was really happening.

She was "The Virgin," but they almost didn't believe her. Yet because she was beautiful and popular and royal, plus there were stories about gods who had human children, there was a possibility that this was true. Nobody knew of any man she could have been with. She and Jared had hidden their relationship well. It would be dangerous to offend a god by asking too many questions if by chance he really had sent this child. It didn't take too long for the story to leak out of Moloch's temple. When King Ahaz found out, he totally disbelieved her story and wanted a trial as soon as she delivered the child. He was in favor of stoning her. He commanded that he be alerted immediately when the baby was born.

Within a month, word reached him that Athaliah had given birth to a son. He rushed to Moloch's temple to confront her. There he found all the priests and priestesses surrounding her bed. When she saw him, she said, "Come father, meet your new grandson. His name is Immanuel" ("God with us" or "gods are with us").

In an instant, Ahaz' anger was changed to shock. There was no way she could have heard about the sign God gave him. He still doubted this was a demigod, but something supernatural had undoubtedly happened. With a cursory glance at her and the baby, he returned to the palace.

Chapter Six:
The Depths of Night

Edomites from south of the Dead Sea had never forgotten the terrible slaughter by King Uzziah's father. During the next year and a half after Immanuel was born, they had enough new soldiers trained to form a strong army. They attacked Judah in the south and carried away a large number of prisoners. This time God did not intervene to bring those people home.

Philistines on the west, by the Mediterranean Sea, attacked time and again and picked off many cities and towns. King Ahaz was confident that the gifts he had sent to Tiglath-Pileser would ensure that he was on his way to help. And help he did. He attacked and captured Damascus, sent the population into exile, and killed Rezin, the king Ahaz had been afraid of. Hoshea had already murdered King Pekah of Israel and become the last king of that doomed nation (2 Kings 15:30). Both kings that Ahaz had feared were gone, just as God had foretold. Did King Ahaz remember that Isaiah had predicted that? There is no evidence that he paid any attention. He sent more gifts because he wanted the Assyrians to destroy more of his enemies.

At one point, King Ahaz even traveled to Damascus to meet King Tiglath-Pileser. While he was there, he saw an altar that he liked. Making a sketch of it with detailed plans for its construction, he sent it to Uriah, the priest of God at the temple in Jerusalem. Uriah had it built according to the plans and finished it before King Ahaz returned. As soon as King Ahaz saw it, he determined to offer sacrifices on it. He offered up his burnt offering and grain offering, poured out his drink offering, and sprinkled the blood of his fellowship offerings on the altar. All of these tasks officially belonged to the priests at the temple, but Uriah was disposed to let King Ahaz do whatever he wanted. At least the king didn't want to go into the Holy Place. He remembered the story of his grandfather, King Uzziah, being struck with leprosy when he presumed to go in there.

Uriah was so willing to let King Ahaz do whatever he wanted that he gave orders for how the offerings were to be made and set about changing all the furniture in the courtyard at the temple. King Ahaz had new plans for the bronze altar that he had replaced. He would use it for seeking guidance. It was tempting to think that the gods were not doing all he asked, and since the Great God had delivered on that promised sign and had destroyed Rezin, the king of Aram (Syria) as He predicted, King Ahaz now thought maybe it would be a good idea to worship at His temple, while still doing things the way he wanted to. He must have envisioned King Tiglath-Pileser coming for a friendly visit, since he arranged the courtyard in deference to the king of Assyria.

During these years, there is some evidence that Hezekiah began to reign with his father, but their views on religion and politics were so divergent that Hezekiah could not have had any power to make a difference in the policies of the government. He had to bide his time and pray that God would give him an opportunity to rule righteously. Hoshea, the last king of Israel was on the throne in Samaria. Aram to the northeast had already been swallowed up by Assyria. The end was not far off for Israel, so they were not actively fighting Judah at this time.

Unfortunately, King Ahaz' hope of receiving help from Assyria did not work out. Assyria gave Ahaz trouble instead of help. In desperation, he stripped the temple of its treasures to send to King Tiglath-Pileser, but that didn't help either. There is no evidence that he received any guidance from the bronze altar. So, he realized, the Great God was not going to help him after all. With that thought, he gathered the gods of Damascus that he had brought home with him, put them in the temple, and began to worship them. He thought, "Since the gods of the kings of Aram have helped them, I will sacrifice to them so they will help me."

One day the high priest of Moloch came to visit King Ahaz. He was very polite and cordial. "Your Majesty," he began. "We have missed you."

King Ahaz nodded his head but didn't say anything. He was waiting to find out the reason for this visit.

"I hear that you have put the gods of Damascus into the temple. It seems to me that they would be uncomfortable in that place. Maybe it is hard for them to answer your prayers from there."

The Depths of Night

Ahaz had not thought of that possibility. Maybe that could explain what was happening. "And what would you suggest I do?"

"Moloch has sent you a message that he would be happy to entertain the gods of Damascus in his courts. That way the gods could all work together to give you a successful reign."

"We could make room for any of the temple furniture you would like to bring with the gods. When everything is set up, we would have a sacred service inaugurating the new day for the kingdom."

"I believe your advice is good. I will think about it overnight and let you know tomorrow." Ahaz pondered the advice the rest of that day and into the evening. What would the priests of Baal think if he followed the advice of the priest of Moloch? The next morning, he went to the temple of Jehovah and announced that all the priests were to return to their own towns. This meant they would be poor, because they would no longer receive the tithes that were given to the temple. He moved out all his gods, then he gathered together the furnishings from the temple of God and took them away. Then he shut and sealed the doors and entrances of the temple. He was going to do more than just move the gods. He was going to do more for the gods than any king of Judah had ever done. He set up altars on every street corner in Jerusalem. In every town in Judah, he built high places to burn sacrifices to other gods (2 Chron. 28:24–25). There were many other idolaters who were happy to help him achieve these plans quickly. And he saved the best for last. He didn't tell one person about his final plan. He knew beyond a shadow of a doubt that the gods were going to help him be more powerful than any other king had ever been.

* * * * *

In Isaiah's house, the family was increasing. Now there were the two daughters, Ruth and Naomi, the first son, Shear-Jashub ("A remnant will return"), and a second son, Maher-Shalal-Hash-Baz ("Quick to the plunder, swift to the spoil"). Maybe no other family on earth has had two sons specifically named by God as predictions of coming events. They and their father Isaiah ("Jehovah saves"), together with the Immanuel sign ("God with us") were all evidence of God's presence, His love for His people, and His control over the circumstances.[16]

---

16   If you would give a pet the name Maher-Shalal-Hash-Baz, you would soon be able to remember what God had said to name Isaiah's second son.

> Maybe no other family on earth has had two sons specifically named by God as predictions of coming events. They and their father Isaiah ("Jehovah saves"), together with the Immanuel sign ("God with us") were all evidence of God's presence.

Anyah was also a regular member of the household. She still had her apartment in the palace, but she was seldom there. With age, she had become much more passive. She had her gardening, her love for Yishka, and her bond with Ruth. She seldom went out now to any kind of worship, even complaining now and then about what was happening in the various temples. Isaiah was not close to her but, after his vision of God, he mentally forgave her for all that had happened during his childhood and youth, and he asked her forgiveness for his former rudeness. She laughed and said he hadn't been that bad. He assured her she was always welcome in his home and, to his surprise, that brought tears to her eyes.

The Prophet Micah continued his work of delivering God's word to Israel and Judah. Isaiah continued to be thankful that God had provided another voice. He did not have the sole burden of giving every message. His responsibilities in the palace were still heavy. And he had the extra task of writing the second set of books and keeping them secretly at home so that ultimately all the truth could be known about what happened during King Ahaz' reign.

One day, a perplexing problem presented itself in Isaiah's house. Yishka received a message. That was unusual enough, but this message was a complete surprise. God told her that King Ahaz planned to sacrifice Immanuel. Since she had no idea who Immanuel was, she had no idea how to proceed. It was mid-morning, and Isaiah was at work. What should she do? With no alternative, she gathered the family to pray about the matter. Anyah came and joined them also. Before praying, Yishka explained the problem. Anyah was appalled that the king would plan such a thing. She didn't even question whether the message was true. After Yishka prayed, Anyah, who knew all the gossip from the temples, explained to her what was happening. Immanuel, who was supposedly a demigod, was the baby that had been born to Athaliah, the high priestess of Moloch.

Apparently, it seemed appropriate to King Ahaz to sacrifice him to that god. That way, Ahaz thought, he would get great honor and power for making such a contribution. That was his final plan that absolutely nobody knew about but himself. Only God could have revealed it to Yishka. Furthermore, it was an emergency because the sacrifice was to be made the next morning.

The next perplexity came in the question of how to deliver the message. Yishka could not go to Moloch's temple. Everyone would know she was not a worshiper there and would question why she was there. How could the message be delivered in such a way that the child could be rescued? The message would have to be delivered before Moloch's temple closed for the night. The little boys didn't understand what they were praying about or hearing. Naomi had a child's understanding. Ruth, who was thirteen years old and was preparing for her engagement party, understood perfectly.

Yishka had prayed, and Anyah had explained, then with a sideways glance at Anyah, Ruth said, "Let me go."

Yishka was shocked! "Why would you say that?" she asked.

With another glance at Anyah who was looking down, she said, "Because I have met Athaliah and she would recognize me."

Yishka got off her knees and stood up. Ruth and Naomi had never seen her angry before. As she walked out of the room, she spoke over her shoulder. "Anyah, come and talk with me." Anyah quickly got up and followed her.

"Did you take Ruth to worship idols?" Yishka asked accusingly after the door was shut between them and the children.

"Not really."

"What do you mean by 'Not really'? You know your son and I made it clear that she was never to go there."

"Let me explain. I think you will feel better. I could never control Isaiah, and I could not control you. When Ruth came, I thought I could control her."

Yishka interrupted, "How is that supposed to make me feel better? Did you think of sacrificing her?"

"No, I swear to you, that thought never crossed my mind. Just let me finish explaining," Anyah said quietly.

"All right. Continue."

"When she was older, sometimes you would let me take her to my apartment in the palace. We would go for her to say 'Hello' to her father, and then I would take her to the temple. She always complained and said people were doing bad things there. She was very perceptive. Finally, I saw what she was talking about. I stopped taking her and I stopped going myself. Now I have not been there for a few years. But before we stopped going, I introduced her to Athaliah since she is a relative."

"And Ruth never said a word about it to any of us!"

"As wise as she was about the temple, I guess she was also smart enough to know it would made you unhappy. I'm sorry now that I took her, but maybe it will work out for the best since she is the only inconspicuous person who can take a message to Athaliah."

Yishka said hesitantly, "Maybe you are right. Let's talk to her." She opened the door and called for Ruth to come.

The three of them discussed what could be done. It was soon decided that Ruth could wear a simple gown with a scarf over her head and walk into the temple without being recognized. She took along her younger brother's oldest play clothes so she could put them on Immanuel and carry him out of Moloch's temple. They decided she should tell Athaliah to come to their house as soon as the temple closed for the night. They volunteered Isaiah to wait for her at a certain corner and guide her to the house. Yishka sent along an outfit that Athaliah could wear. It would be disastrous for her to leave in her priestess apparel. Since nobody at the temple had been alerted to King Ahaz' plan, she could probably get out with little trouble, but it would be dangerous if anyone followed her.

Yishka watched with a catch in her throat as her older daughter set out alone on this dangerous errand. Then she and Anyah spent the time in prayer until she returned.

Following other simple-looking women into the temple was no problem, but how was she to find Athaliah? Keeping her scarf low over her forehead, Ruth looked around for any sign of the high priestess. Meanwhile, she prayed silently that God would help her succeed. About two minutes after she entered the temple, she saw Athaliah moving from her room to another part of the temple. Hurrying without running, she spoke softly, "Athaliah."

Athaliah turned to see who had spoken her name. Nobody looked familiar. Ruth approached her and said, "I'm Ruth. Do you remember me?"

Curious, Athaliah looked closely at her and said, "Yes, I do remember you. But you never came here looking this way. Where is your grandmother?"

"She is at home with my mother. I'm here on an emergency mission. I have to speak to you privately. I cannot be recognized by anyone else."

Puzzled, but wanting to be polite, Athaliah walked with Ruth through a maze of passageways to the back door to her apartment. Immanuel was playing on the floor. What a good-looking little boy he was!

In a rush, her words tumbled out as Ruth gave the message and delivered the instructions. She wanted to leave the temple as quickly as possible.

Athaliah turned pale and began to tremble. Immanuel was all she had. She could not lose him. She didn't stop to question the message. It sounded too much like something her father would think of doing. Quickly they changed Immanuel's beautiful clothes for the grimy ones Ruth had brought. They rubbed a little dirt on his face as the finishing touch.

Wrapping him in her scarf, Ruth repeated the directions one more time and walked with Immanuel out the back door. Athaliah directed her to a less obvious way to leave the temple compound. Immanuel waved his little hand and said, "Bye, Mommy." It tore at Athaliah's heart! Would she ever see him again?

When Isaiah arrived home that evening, he found three little boys playing in the garden instead of just his two. Yishka filled him in on the day's events, as well as the conversation with Anyah. It was hard for him to feel happy, but he admitted that the women had done the only possible thing. If more was to be said about it, it would have to come later. While he waited for supper, he picked up Immanuel and played with him for a few minutes. He was a well-behaved, sweet little boy. Here was the amazing answer to the sign that God had given King Ahaz. He felt awed by the thought: "God with Us."

He readily agreed to go to the assigned spot and wait to accompany his great-niece to their house. Yishka told him which garment she had sent, so he would recognize it even if he couldn't recognize Athaliah. He added one detail. He took along Ruel so the two men could chat while they waited. That would be less conspicuous than a solitary man waiting on the corner.

Soon after the appointed time, a simple-looking woman approached the corner. Seeing the two men, she hesitated. Recognizing the dress, Isaiah moved toward her and quietly said he would see her safely home to her family. Bidding his father-in-law goodnight, he started with her toward home. Seeing that she was trembling uncontrollably, he gently took her elbow and guided her home. She was afraid she was going to faint, but his hand gave her comfort and support. The moment they were through the door, she saw Immanuel and burst into tears. Immanuel repeatedly said, "No, Mommy. Don't cry." Finally, he began to cry also, and that helped her to dry her tears.

She laughed and said, "No, Immanuel. Don't cry." Then he could laugh as well.

After Yishka had served her some supper and the three boys had been put to bed, Isaiah sat down to talk to Athaliah. She was safe now, but he wasn't sure about tomorrow morning when the temple discovered that she and the child had disappeared. And what would happen when King Ahaz arrived to announce his sacrifice of the child? There were questions she would have to answer tonight so they could make the best possible plans.

Isaiah asked her how she happened to give the name *Immanuel* to her son. She explained about him supposedly being a demigod, so it seemed like the logical name. Isaiah asked if she had heard the name anywhere else. No, she had not. So, he told her the story of the message to her father which included the sign of a mature young woman having a baby and naming it *Immanuel*. Athaliah was awestruck! The Great God had named her son! She was an agnostic idolater, but the Great God had named her son! She couldn't get over it. That would explain why her angry father did not have her stoned.

Isaiah talked to her as if they were equals. When he asked her about Immanuel's father, she responded by asking him why he doubted that she, a virgin, had borne the child who had come from a god. His answer stunned her. When God had given him the sign for her father, He had used the word for *a mature young woman*, not the specific word that meant *a virgin*. So, he repeated, it was appropriate to ask her about the child's father. He was certainly not asking so she could be stoned. He was asking because he didn't think it would be safe for her to stay in his house for the long term. She surely could not go back to the temple or the palace. Where could she go? Maybe the father or his family could take her in and hide her.

She had never been able to cry for the loss of Jared. Now the tears tumbled out and overflowed. Isaiah patted her arm and waited for her to regain her composure. When she was finally able to pull herself together, she gave him the whole story. His heart was touched by her sadness. He decided then and there that he would try to locate Jared's mother. Athaliah knew the names of Jared's father and mother—Eliel and Jerusha—but had never heard where they lived. Since they were godly people, it was possible that some of the righteous men Isaiah had studied with would know something about that family.

The next morning King Ahaz rose early and, ceremoniously with a contingent of guards, proceeded to the temple of Moloch. As the king approached, the priests and priestesses gathered to welcome him. That was the first time anyone noticed that The Virgin was not among them. Someone rushed to call her before the king could notice her absence. She was not in her apartment; she was not performing the ceremonies she usually presided over in the morning. And then the king was there, and it was too late to spend more time looking.

With great seriousness and pomp, the king announced that he had decided to honor Moloch by giving him the very best. He would sacrifice the demigod child that Moloch had honored their city by sending to them. It was fitting to give the demigod to the god. And now the baby was to be brought forth. But shockingly, there was no baby. Those who had looked for The Virgin had seen that the little boy was missing as well.

The Depths of Night

Nothing could stem the king's anger as this news was cautiously given. How could Athaliah have disappeared? She could not possibly have known his plans. Who saw her last? Who saw the child last? Had her apartment been searched for evidence? The response was that the day before had been perfectly normal. Nobody had seen anything out of the ordinary. Her apartment had been searched already this morning, and everything was in perfect order. She and the baby could not have been victims of violence.

> *The king announced that he had decided to honor Moloch by giving him the very best. He would sacrifice the demigod child that Moloch had honored their city by sending to them. It was fitting to give the demigod to the god.*

As this exchange was taking place, the high priest secretly sent a priestess to search the apartment again to see what she could find. The people who had been there before had not searched thoroughly, because they did not know there was a need to do such a thing. But that could not be told to the king.

Meanwhile the king continued ranting, moving on to blaming the temple for such lax discipline that a woman could wander off whenever she wanted to. The high priest was trying to pacify King Ahaz. He explained that The Virgin had been in charge of all the other priestesses. She had been so careful and thorough in her work that nobody had ever suspected that she needed watching. She had been a credit to her father, the king.

That idea enraged him even more. By now, he was spewing venom without a thought as to how his words might be interpreted. He revealed just how useless and worthless he thought this daughter had been to him. His audience gasped as they compared his estimation of her with their own high esteem of her. Now every person who could hear him was glad she had escaped with her little boy. Suddenly none of them had any intention of revealing anything they might find that would help him locate her or bring the child back to be sacrificed. Two or three silently moved away from the group to go to The Virgin's apartment to tell the searcher not to find a single thing.

His vitriol crescendoed as the audience around him slowly backed away. This was the king. Who knew what he might do? Suddenly his voice stilled, his face slowly lost its angry look, and he slumped to the floor. His guards rushed around him, trying to see what had happened. He was alive, but it was obvious he would not be able to get up. His body twitched in abnormal movements. The chief guard talked to him, asking if he could speak, if he could move. It was not clear whether he heard, but he could not respond in any of the requested ways. The guards cleared the crowd that had gathered, and told the high priest to close the temple. Several guards were sent racing back to the palace to bring a litter. As soon as it arrived, they carefully placed the king on it, and carried him back to the palace to his own bed.

Moloch's temple could open again. Now it was without a high priestess and with uncertainty about the status of the king. It was a solemn day of anguish as everyone waited to find out what would happen next.

At the palace, one of the guards was anxious to relate exactly what had happened at Moloch's temple. As a result, just as much uncertainty was felt there. After hearing the information, Isaiah stole a few minutes to rush home and relate that the urgency to move Athaliah and Immanuel from the house was toned down for the moment.

The co-ruler Hezekiah was notified to visit his father and then be available at all times, as the attendants waited to see what would happen to King Ahaz. Hezekiah found his father unable to speak, although he did try to make sounds. He was also unable to swallow. He had not yet reached forty years of age. Several attendants noted that he was very young to have this happen to him. Whether young or not, it had happened. The next morning, he was no better. In fact, he was worse, because he had not been able to take either food or drink.

King Ahaz lingered for three days and then died. His son, Hezekiah, was immediately proclaimed the sole king. He, together with the leadership of the kingdom, including Isaiah, decided not to bury Ahaz with the kings. He had done too much harm to the country. Instead, they found somewhere else in the city of Jerusalem to place his body.

Yishka had wondered through the years why God had given her so few messages. The past few days had laid that concern to rest. The main task He had given her was to help Isaiah. With the heavy burdens he bore, it was essential that he have a home where he could escape the pressures that surrounded him and find peace and rest. She had provided that, faithfully loving and caring for him and supporting him in every way in his prophetic work. In addition, from time to time, she had been directed to warn or encourage someone else. Now she could clearly see that God had guided and helped her as much as He had her husband. He had helped her rear a lovely family who all served and worshiped God. He didn't keep her so busy that she had little time for her home and family. Now He had used her to save the little child who represented God's presence among His people. She could pray with heartfelt honesty that it was enough. God had treated her in just the right way. At last, she had no lingering sense of being ignored or bypassed.

That same year, God gave a message to the prophet Isaiah concerning the Philistines. For years they had been harassing Judah, capturing one town after another. Many, including Jared's family, had lost their property to them. This message must have been a comfort to those faithful to God. It is found in Isaiah 14:28–32.

It begins by warning the Philistines not to rejoice that King Ahaz was dead. A far worse enemy was coming and that was Assyria, followed by Babylon. They would soon be subjugated under the violence of one kingdom and then the other. God's people would lie down in safety, but those who rebelled against God would not share that fate. The only safe place was under God's care. Those who rejected Him would be rejecting His ability to care for them.

PART IV:

Hezekiah, the King[17]

---

[17] The stories from the time of King Hezekiah are found in 2 Kings 18–20; 2 Chronicles, chapters 29 to 32; and in Isaiah chapters 36 to 39.

Chapter Seven:

The Dawn of a Bright New Morning

Hezekiah came to the throne determined to do all in his power to save Judah from the fate that was overtaking the northern kingdom. Assyria had besieged Samaria for three years, then carried thousands into captivity. The same thing could happen to Judah if God didn't work mightily on their behalf.

His first project was to restore the temple services which had been shut down for the last few years of Ahaz' reign. First, he called for a loyal group of priests and Levites to return to Jerusalem from their homes throughout Judah. Then he convinced them of his plans. The priests began work at once, cleaning and sanctifying the temple. They sent word to many others to come and help. Because of the years of desecration and neglect, it was a difficult job that required many skilled artisans and craftsmen.

The gates and doors were opened and repaired. Thorough cleaning took place. The furniture that Ahaz had removed was located and moved back into the original locations. The temple vessels had to be located and polished, and many of them were made anew, because Ahaz had sent many to King Tiglath-Pileser. Idols had been worshiped in the sacred space; therefore, special ceremonies were conducted to cleanse the temple of unholy influences.

> *The priests began work at once, cleaning and sanctifying the temple. They sent word to many others to come and help. Because of the years of desecration and neglect, it was a difficult job.*

Meanwhile, Isaiah's house was bursting at the seams. Athaliah and Immanuel had settled into the family's routines. The three little boys had a wonderful time together. Athaliah was exceptionally polite and helpful. Anyah especially was proud of her for not acting like a princess while she was being cared for in a busy household. Ruel knew about Athaliah since he had waited for her with Isaiah on the street corner, and Isaiah told Ruel what he had learned after his long conversation with Athaliah. The two men felt that, under the circumstances, the immorality of what she had done should not be held against her. Her whole life had been lived in an environment of immorality. Both men began doing their best to make cautious inquiries about Jared's family.

The work being done on the temple was completed within less than a month. Everything was ready for the re-establishment of the sanctuary services. In the first service held, the king and the rulers of the city together with the priests and Levites began the worship service by making many sacrifices and seeking forgiveness for the sins of the nation. Then, for the first time in years, the temple courts resounded with words of praise and adoration. The music of King David and Asaph, his music director, was sung with great joy! Trumpets and cymbals and harps and lyres accompanied the singing.

When the wonderful day of worship was over, the next item on King Hezekiah's agenda was to hold a Passover. He sent out word to all Israel and Judah, as well as letters to Ephraim and Manasseh. In the past, all twelve tribes had traveled three times each year to Jerusalem to worship together. King Hezekiah determined to do his best to see that take place again. Because the temple and the priests weren't prepared yet, they decided to celebrate Passover a month later than usual. The king and all the assembly were working together on this. They sent the announcement from Dan to Beersheba, the traditional northern and southern points of the previously united kingdom. Couriers carried the message everywhere, "Come to Jerusalem and celebrate the Passover to the Lord, the God of Israel."

The last king of Israel was hemmed in in Samaria because Assyria was besieging that capital city, so it was easy for the couriers to travel throughout the land. Many, over the next few years and beyond, would be taken captive, but at that time many people still remained there in the smaller towns and on their farms. The confirmed idol worshipers in Israel mostly scorned and ridiculed the couriers' news. A few people from the tribes of Asher, Manasseh, and Zebulun humbled themselves and journeyed to Jerusalem. Ultimately some also came from the tribes of Ephraim and Issachar. A very large crowd of people assembled in Jerusalem to celebrate the Feast of Unleavened Bread. Before the services began, the whole crowd went through the streets of Jerusalem, utterly destroying the altars and images that Ahaz had set up. They threw all the debris into the Kidron Valley. When they came to the temples of Baal and Moloch, they found them abandoned. Word had spread about what was happening. Knowing the stories from the past, the priests and priestesses disappeared. There was no one left to interfere with the task of uniting the city in the worship of God.

Many priests and Levites were just then coming back into Jerusalem from their small tracts of land. They had all been forced to leave when the temple closed. Now they rushed to purify themselves and resume the responsibilities they had had before. They quickly relearned their roles in the ceremonies. Many of the visitors from the north had not properly purified themselves; they were not ritually clean. When this came to the attention of the authorities, King Hezekiah prayed for them and they were able to participate in the service with God's blessing.

In Isaiah's house, there was great joy that God had remembered His people and that restoration of the temple had taken place so quickly. Everyone but Athaliah was looking forward to the Passover. She was afraid to leave the house for fear someone would recognize her. Consequently, she stayed home with the three little boys and Naomi. Ruth was old enough to join with the adults in the celebration. Isaiah and Yishka made it known to everyone they could trust that they were looking for Jerusha, the widow of Eliel. Only Ruel knew why they were searching for her. With the huge crowds in Jerusalem, there was a good chance she would be there, but finding her would take a miracle.

The Dawn of a Bright New Morning

For seven days the Passover was celebrated with great rejoicing. Every day there was sacrificing and teaching and singing, accompanied by the Lord's instruments of praise. At the close of the week, the whole congregation wanted to continue the joyful celebration for another seven days to learn more fully the way of the Lord. There had not been a Passover like this since the days of King Solomon.

One day, during the Passover, Athaliah heard some commotion in the garden. Cautiously she peaked out to see what was going on. An older lady, very thin and tired looking, was crying. The three boys were trying to cheer her up. Athaliah hurried out to join the group. Seeing her, the lady struggled to control her tears.

> *For seven days the Passover was celebrated with great rejoicing. Every day there was sacrificing and teaching and singing, accompanied by the Lord's instruments of praise.*

"May I ask why you are crying?" questioned Athaliah.

"Someone named Yishka told me to come here and meet those who live here," she said through her tears.

"And why does that make you sad?"

"Because years ago, I had a little boy who looked just like this," she said, pointing to Immanuel.

Light began to dawn for Athaliah. "Is your name Jerusha?"

Controlling her tears, she said, "Yes, it is. How would you know?"

"Because Jared told me his mother's name was Jerusha."

"Who are you, and how do you know Jared?"

"Let me tell you first that this young boy is named Immanuel, and he is the son of Jared."

Jerusha began to cry again. "My son has a son? I have a grandchild? How can it be? Who is the mother?"

"It is a long story. Come inside where we can talk. But first let me introduce you. Boys, this is Immanuel's grandmother."

"Isn't my grandmother also Immanuel's grandmother," asked Shear-Jashub.

"No, she is Immanuel's auntie."

"But we are still all one family, right?"

"Absolutely. We are all one family." Athaliah had never felt so much a part of this family until she said it. With the saying, she realized that this was the most important family she had ever been a part of.

Leaving the boys to their play, the two women went into the house to visit.

Athaliah asked Jerusha when she had last heard from Jared. Her answer made it clear that she did not know what had happened to him. Athaliah sighed heavily and wondered where to start. Finally, she said, "I am Immanuel's mother. My name is Athaliah."

Jerusha winced at that name, but she hugged Athaliah, and said, "Bless you, bless you, my daughter-in-law." It was still hard to know where to go in the conversation from there. Hesitantly, Athaliah started at the beginning when she first met Jared and truthfully continued through all the twists and turns of the story. Jerusha gasped and cried again when she heard how Jared had died. Athaliah cried with her. Later, she related how Yishka, the prophetess, had received the message which saved her son from death. She told how Ruth came to deliver the message and get Immanuel out of the temple, then how she escaped to this house. She finished with telling how the king's stroke had saved her and Immanuel from being hunted and killed. Then Athaliah said, "Ever since then, we have been trying to find you so you could know about Jared and meet your grandson."

Jerusha was hardly without tears through the whole story. Then she said, "Now that we have found each other, can we find a way to stay together? I know that you and Isaiah the prophet are members of the royal family, but I am not."

"Being royal does not matter. Isaiah's father was not royal, and his wife is not royal. I have not been associated with the royal family since I was ten years old. But now that my father Ahaz is gone, I think my brother King Hezekiah will welcome me again."

"You don't want to stay in this house? I can only imagine living in the house of Isaiah the prophet."

"We are only here because it was the safest place for us to come. By now I love this family and this house, but we are making them very crowded. We have been waiting to find you before deciding where I should go with Immanuel. If you will have me, I want to be with you. Where do you live?"

"Unfortunately, since I lost contact with Jared, I have had to live on charity from other people. Now I am in a tiny little place, far too small for the three of us."

"In that case, I am going to visit King Hezekiah. He will not refuse to help his sister and her family. I will ask Isaiah to go with me tonight. Now that my father is dead and the temples are abandoned, I am feeling somewhat safer. Of course, many of the Great God worshippers will want to stone me for having a baby out of wedlock."

Jerusha said, "Didn't you feel married to Jared?"

"Actually, I did. He was the only man I ever cared about or touched."

"Well, there you are," said Jerusha with a satisfied smile. "Who is there to say you were not married to him?"

"Nobody, I guess. Now that everyone has left the temples, but somebody could show up later."

"There is a Jewish tradition that if a man says a child is his, nobody is to question it. I think it is my right to speak for my son. I, as your mother-in-law, will definitely say you were married, and Immanuel is my grandson.

With a laugh, Athaliah hugged Jerusha.

Later that night, Isaiah accompanied Athaliah to speak with her brother. They had not met in years, but each of them had suffered through life with their father, and they were unspeakably happy to see each other. They rejoiced in the fact that both of them had survived to meet again. King Hezekiah knew just the apartment that would be perfect for three people. They could move in any time. Hesitantly, the king made one request. With the Passover proceeding so well and with the new determination in the kingdom to worship only the God of Heaven, would it be possible for Athaliah to change her name? He realized she was not to blame for having it, but now that things were different, she would get along better with a different name. Athaliah had actually been thinking that herself, and it didn't take long for her to suggest an alternative.

"Immanuel and I are safe because of Yishka the prophetess. Would it be presumptuous of me to take the name of another prophetess, Deborah?"

Hezekiah immediately replied, "I think it is a very appropriate name for you! After all, your child is a sign from God and a reminder to all of us that He is with us."

Then she confessed to him that she had not believed in any god/God since she went to the temple, but now that she had seen God work wonders to name Immanuel, then save them, and then bring Jerusha into their lives, she could not possibly disbelieve in God. She was looking forward to becoming better acquainted with Him.

> *Then she confessed to him that she had not believed in any god/God since she went to the temple, but now that she had seen God work wonders to name Immanuel, then save them, and then bring Jerusha into their lives, she could not possibly disbelieve in God.*

It was difficult to remove Immanuel from his playmates but, with promises of lots of play dates both here and inside the palace, the family of three was comfortably settled in just a few days.

With a scarf pulled well over her head, Deborah attended the last couple of days of the Passover with Jerusha and received the final blessing the priest bestowed on those who had attended. It was evident that God had wrought marvelously for the conversion of backsliding Judah and in stemming the tide of idolatry which had threatened to sweep everything before it.

When the final ceremonies closed, those returning home took an active part in an important work which remained to be done. Throughout Judah and Benjamin and in Ephraim and Manasseh, they smashed the sacred stones and cut down the Asherah poles. They cut down the groves and destroyed the high places and altars (2 Chron. 31:1). After they had destroyed all of them, those of both the north and south parted from each other, and the Israelites returned to their own towns and to their own property.

The third item on King Hezekiah's agenda was to reorganize all the priests and Levites into groups with specific duties. For years, they had lived without an income from the tithe. Now the king announced to the people living in Jerusalem that they should begin again to give the portion due the priests and Levites so they could devote themselves to the Law of the Lord. As soon as the directive went out, the Israelites generously gave the firstfruits of their grain, new wine, oil, and honey and all that the fields produced. They brought a great amount, a tithe of everything. The men of Israel and Judah who lived in the other towns of Judah also brought a tithe of their herds and flocks and a tithe of the holy things dedicated to the Lord their God, and they stacked them in groups. They began doing this the month after the Passover and didn't finish bringing the tithe until four months later. They had waited for years to again have the opportunity to return what belonged to the Lord. When King Hezekiah and his officials, including Isaiah, came and saw the heaps, they praised God and blessed His people, Israel.

The king asked the priests and Levites about the piles of gifts and learned that they were just the leftovers after everyone had received as much as they could use. So, Hezekiah gave orders to prepare storerooms in the temple of the Lord, and this was done. Then the various contributions could be stored with duly appointed men to take care of them.

They also set up a system whereby all the males from three years old and up whose names were in the genealogical records of the priests and Levites would receive regular allotments. All priests and Levites from twenty years old and up were paid according to their responsibilities. All the priests who were descended from Aaron and lived outside Jerusalem were designated by name to distribute portions to every male among them, to all who were recorded in the genealogies of the Levites.

It was seen that King Hezekiah was determined to undo all the damage his father had done. Because he trusted in God, he was very successful. Throughout his reign a series of remarkable providences revealed to the surrounding nations that the God of Israel was with His people.

One aftermath of the Passover was the influx of refugees from Israel. Having been there for the Passover and having experienced life in a city committed to righteousness, those who were loyal to God wanted to escape from the idolatry of the Israelites and from the Assyrians who were continuing to raid and take people captive. King Hezekiah welcomed them and helped them find places where they could fit into Judah's society. Tabitha, the little girl captive, found a loving husband among these new citizens. The prophecy about her was fulfilled and, throughout her life, she thanked God for all He had done to restore her soul.

* * * * *

During Ahaz' final years and King Hezekiah's early years, God sent several messages through the prophet Isaiah that all centered around the sign of Immanuel, "God with us." Beginning in Chapter 7, God gave the sign to Ahaz, even though he did not want it. In Chapter 8, Isaiah warns that Assyria would definitely attack Judah as few were faithful to God, and so many were worshipping idols. And yet, God would be with them. No matter how many rejected Him, those who feared God should not follow the way of the apostates. They should only consult God and wait on Him for salvation.

Chapter 9 looked to the future when the long-awaited Messiah, the true Immanuel, would come. God himself would rule over an everlasting kingdom with justice and righteousness. Those who do not welcome Him will end up destroying themselves. In chapter 10, disaster will come for those who only care about themselves and ignore the rights of the poor and widows and orphans. In the days to come, they will have even less than the people whose needs they ignored. God will punish the Assyrians for thinking it is their own wisdom that allows them to conquer the world. They think their gods are better than all the other gods of the countries they have defeated. They think that, since the gods of so many countries have not been able to withstand their armies, the God of Israel will be no different. The king of Assyria said, "I've done all this. It has been by my wisdom and understanding. I can take more countries as easily as I could take eggs out of an abandoned nest, without anyone flapping a wing or opening its mouth to chirp."

God likens Assyria to an ax, a saw, a rod, and a club. All of them can be deadly weapons, but they have to be used by someone with a strong arm. God had been the one who had permitted Assyria to gain so much strength. However, Assyria had arrogantly claimed more than can be attributed to just human ability. God allowed them to wage war in order to wake up godless nations, but their brutality and violence had gone beyond anything God could allow—because He is always on the side of victims. Now He foretells that Assyria will be punished and reduced in size until a child could count the number of the remaining soldiers. Those who were loyal to God should not be afraid of the Assyrians. God will deal with them, as He did the Midianites and the Egyptians. To God's people, that warning brought to mind familiar stories about God's care in the past.

Chapter 12 is a glorious song of praise to the God Who is with us. "This hymn of praise brings to a close what has been called the 'Immanuel Volume' of Isaiah's prophecies."[18]

---

18 *Seventh-day Adventist Bible Commentary, Volume 4: Isaiah to Malachi* (Washington, DC: Review and Herald Publishing Association, 1955), p. 135.

Chapter Eight:
One Big Mistake

In the middle of King Hezekiah's prosperous reign, he was suddenly stricken with a fatal malady. He had a boil, and it must have been a particularly bad infection. If you have ever had a boil, you will be able to sympathize with him. Boils produce fever and intense pain, and they almost always have to be cut open so the pus can be drained. Even today, boils require antibiotics to combat the infection which threatens to overwhelm the body. Of course, that treatment was not available in Hezekiah's day. At first, the king must have hoped he would soon be well but, when the prophet Isaiah came, the last hope was gone because his message was, "You will die."

It hardly seemed fair that he should die so young when he had worked harder than any other king of Judah to revive the spiritual life and rebuild the prestige of the kingdom and of the city. His son Manasseh was too young to take his place. Plus, the nation was living under the threat of invasion by Assyria. With no other option in view, the king turned his face to the wall and wept bitterly and pleaded with God for more time to live.

Before Isaiah had time to walk out of the palace, God gave him a different message. "Go back and tell Hezekiah, the leader of My people, 'This is what the Lord, the God of your father David, says, 'I have heard your prayer and seen your tears; I will heal you. On the third day from now you will go up to the temple of the Lord. I will add fifteen years to your life. And I will deliver you and this city from the hand of the king of Assyria. I will defend this city for my sake and for the sake of My servant David.'"

What joy this answer to the prayer brought to both Hezekiah and Isaiah!

Isaiah directed the attending servants to prepare a poultice of figs and put it on the boil. And sure enough, that worked, and Hezekiah recovered.

The king had asked the prophet, "What will be the sign that the Lord will heal me and that I will go up to the temple of the Lord on the third day from now?"

Isaiah responded to his question by asking him to make a choice between having the shadow cast by the sun go forward ten steps on King Ahaz' stairway or having the sunlight go back ten steps.

Hezekiah did not take long to make a choice. He said it would be a simple matter for the shadow to go forward, so he chose for the sign to be the shadow going backward ten steps.

Isaiah immediately prayed that God would perform this sign, and the two men watched as the shadow on the stairway receded backward ten steps. Think what that meant! How did that happen? Were the tides shifted? Was the earth slowed in its revolution? How many stars and/or other planets would have been affected? It was mind-boggling to King Hezekiah! He wrote a profound poem prayer of wonder and thanksgiving about what happened to him and what God had done for him. You can read it in Isaiah 38:

He has spoken to me, and he himself has done this.

I will walk humbly all my years....

You restored me to health and let me live....

In your love you kept me from the pit of destruction;

One Big Mistake

You have put all my sins behind your back....

Those who go down to the pit [of death] cannot hope for your faithfulness. The living, the living—they praise you, as I am doing today.

Fathers tell their children about your faithfulness

The Lord will save me, and we will sing with stringed instruments all the days of our lives in the temple of the LORD.

Maybe if King Hezekiah had repeated this poem prayer every day; maybe if he had gathered his children, including Manasseh, around him as he mentioned in the poem, and talked at length with them about what God had done; maybe if he had turned this into a hymn he and his family really could sing in the temple; maybe if he had pleaded with God to keep him from temptation with as much fervor as he had pleaded for healing—maybe then he would not have made his big mistake.

Seven hundred miles straight across the desert was Babylon. But the desert was too dry and hot for anyone to travel that way. Instead, it was a one-thousand-seven-hundred-mile trip by road. Babylon had had an interesting past. In King Hezekiah's time, it was an unimportant city, but not for long. Isaiah had already prophesied that it would rise in importance again and be a mighty empire. Despite its current political weakness, it was the foremost city in the world for the study of astronomy and other sciences.

Those Babylonian astronomers noticed to their amazement that the shadow on their sundial had turned back ten degrees. That fact became a matter of intense discussion. Eventually someone heard that this was done as a sign to the king of Judah that the God of heaven had granted him a new lease on life. Because of the distance involved in getting the information to Babylon, the astronomers learned this some months after the sign happened.

King MerodachBaladan (also known as *Marduk-Baladan* because Marduk was the main god) of Babylon sent a group of high officials to congratulate Hezekiah on his recovery. Also, more importantly, they were eager to learn about a God who could perform so great a wonder, something far more supernatural than anything they had ever imagined.

What a perfect witnessing opportunity for Hezekiah. He could have told them his story. He could have taught them the song so they could all sing it together. He could have welcomed their questions and asked the prophet Isaiah to help him answer them.

Sadly, none of that happened. Pride took over. He probably thought to himself that they were from a lowly backwater nation that could do Judah no harm. Also, they were enemies of Assyria so, in a way, they were allies of his. Little did he know what ultimate folly it was to make them aware of the riches of his nation. He totally forgot to tell them to glorify God for what He had done.

God was testing him, though he didn't know it. He failed the test by magnifying himself instead of God.

God revealed to Isaiah that the returning delegation was carrying with them a report of the riches they had seen. He was shown that they and their king would make a plan to come back and appropriate all of this. We can only imagine how Isaiah felt when he heard this. Hezekiah had been the best king since Uzziah—even better. And now suddenly his bad judgment had ruined the kingdom. It must have been a difficult task for Isaiah to go and confront him. What could he say?

He started out by asking about the strangers who had come. What did they say? Where were they from?

"From a distant land," said Hezekiah. "They came to me from Babylon."

"What did they see in your palace?" asked Isaiah.

Hezekiah's response was totally naïve. He seemed delighted to boast about what he had done. "They saw everything in my palace. There is nothing among my treasures that I did not show them."

Then Isaiah had to deliver the prophecy that would come about as a consequence of Hezekiah's actions. "Hear the word of the LORD Almighty: The time will surely come when everything in your palace, and all that your fathers have stored up until this day, will be carried off to Babylon. Nothing will be left, says the LORD. And some of your descendants, your own flesh and blood who will be born to you, will be taken away, and they will become officials in the palace of the king of Babylon."

Isaiah must have expected instant remorse and repentance from the king for what he had done. Instead, he was shocked by what King Hezekiah actually said. "At least there will be peace and truth in my days. The word of the Lord which you have spoken is good!" What utter selfishness! What lack of comprehension!

Fortunately, after some period of soul-searching, King Hezekiah did repent of his actions and humbled himself for his pride of heart. In fact, he confessed to the inhabitants of Jerusalem what he had done, and all of them together humbled themselves before the Lord. God graciously accepted their confessions and, as He had promised, did not bring disaster upon them in the days of Hezekiah. In a way, the prideful king's big mistake led to a revival of godliness

One Big Mistake

in Jerusalem. For the rest of his life, the king's steadfast purpose was to redeem the past and to bring honor to the name of God. Tremendous trials lay ahead, and he learned that the only way to triumph over the powers of darkness that plotted his ruin and the total destruction of God's people was to put his trust fully in the Holy One of Israel.

You and I can learn an important lesson from his mistake. Even after a wonderful experience with the Lord, if we neglect to invite Him daily to guide us, we are in danger of falling into Satan's trap and glorifying ourselves instead of God. Let's remember Isaiah 26:12 and review it often: "LORD, you establish peace for us; all that we have accomplished you have done for us." We have the privilege of working with God, and He is the only one who can make good things happen. May we choose to put our lives in God's hands every morning, letting Him guide our choices and decisions. "Consecrate yourself to God in the morning. Make this your very first work. Let your prayer be, 'Take me, O Lord, as wholly thine. I lay all my plans at Your feet. Use me today in Thy service.'"[19] In this way, we can avoid making a big mistake that would surely bring bad consequences. The consequences would not come from God. They would come from the devil who is watching for an opportunity to catch us at a time when we are not depending on God to watch over us. That would give the devil an opportunity to hurt us or other people—or maybe a whole nation.

For the rest of King Hezekiah's life, he had great prosperity. His unwavering purpose to stay close to God made it possible for God to bless him in every conceivable way. Other than his one big mistake, he lived his life in harmony with God. And God led him to prosper in all his works. This shows us how gracious God is to forgive and bless those who repent and turn to him. In one of the chapters ahead, we have an even more amazing story of God's forgiveness. But even with forgiveness, it is not always possible for all the consequences of sin to be avoided.

---

19   White, Ellen G. *Steps to Christ*. Mountain View, CA: Pacific Press Publishing Association, 1892, p. 70.1.

Chapter Nine:
Prophecies of Disaster

In his writing, Isaiah's attention is now directed to surrounding nations, which he focuses on in Chapters 13 through 23. His messages were borne, not primarily to the people mentioned in them, but to God's people, in order that they might understand what would happen to the nations about them. He began with Babylon in chapters 13 into 14. It is very clear that the country and the city would come to its end. The Medes are mentioned as the ones who will overthrow it (Isa. 13:1, 17). In Isaiah's time, the Median kingdom was insignificant. Also, the Persians were hardly known in those days. Yet this prophecy forecasts that together they would become a world empire.

In the patriarchal period, the time of Abraham, Isaac and Jacob, Babylon had been a great power of the Orient. About 800 years before the time of Isaiah, it passed into a state of eclipse, while such nations as Egypt, Assyria, and the Hittite empire occupied dominant places in Near Eastern Affairs. In Isaiah's day, though a vassal kingdom of Assyria, Babylon was beginning to regain its lost power and, within another century, was again to be the outstanding nation of Western Asia. Throughout its ups and downs of political power over the years, it was always considered a headquarters of pagan religion.

After becoming the golden kingdom, Babylon would finally be destroyed, never to be rebuilt. It took centuries for this to happen. During King Hezekiah's lifetime, King Sennacherib of Assyria utterly demolished Babylon, but his son, Esarhaddon, rebuilt it before the time of Daniel. Over centuries, it gradually diminished, until, during the reign of Roman emperor Trajan (A.D. 98–117), after Jesus had lived on earth, it was a complete ruin. God's people would not need to fear Babylon even though they would be captive there. God had told them far in advance what would happen to Babylon.

In chapter 14, Isaiah introduces one of his favorite themes: the great ingathering of people from all nations to the worship and service of the true God. Had the Jews diligently served the Lord upon their return from Babylon, it was His plan that they would finally rule the world. All men would have recognized one another as brethren. All would have worshipped the Lord and rejoiced in His salvation. Since the people of Judah rebelled against God, He had to go to Plan B. Now we look forward to the people of God finding rest in the New Earth.

Isaiah presents a parable in highly figurative language. Babylon is pictured as being greeted in the grave by many other leaders who had already died. They welcome Babylon with the taunt that he had become weak, as they are. He had become like them. But at least they were on thrones. All Babylon's pomp has arrived at the grave and has been thrown down and covered with maggots and worms (Isa. 14: 9–11).

Next, Babylon is equated with Satan before he was cast out of heaven, when he was second only to Christ in power and authority and was the head of the angelic hosts until his fall. "How you have fallen from heaven, morning star, son of the dawn! You have been cast down to the earth, you who once laid low the nations! You said in your heart, 'I will ascend to the heavens; I will raise my throne above the stars of God …. I will make myself like the Most High.' But you are brought down to the realm of the dead, to the depths of the pit." Read this whole section from verses 12 through 20. After Satan—the name we know him by—is dead, everyone will look in amazement at him, remembering what he did during his time on earth. This is the first mention in the Bible that there is a powerful angel behind all evil.

Isaiah foretold that the location of Babylon would become a place for owls to burrow. Babylon, the jewel of kingdoms, would never again be inhabited or lived in through all generations (Isa. 14:22–23). Many centuries later in 1983, Saddam Hussein, dictator of Iraq, decided to challenge that prophecy. He believed himself to be descended from Nebuchadnezzar, and he determined to rebuild Babylon and reign there. If you know your history, you know what happened to that ambition.

A short pronouncement about Assyria follows the long message about Babylon. Judah's current enemy was Assyria. King Sennacherib of Assyria would invade Judea and threaten to overcome them. But the Lord would break that yoke and deliver His people. Although the whole world stood in awe of Assyrian might, it was nothing to God who has determined the outcome. His hand is stretched out over all nations: Babylon, Assyria, and all others. Who is there that can thwart him? Who can stop Him from doing what He sees best? Isaiah saw the hand of God stretched out over all nations and trusted that His plans would come to pass.

In chapters 15, 16, Isaiah then reveals that Moab would suffer the fate of other kingdoms as Assyria conquered them. Ruin, destruction, wailing, and weeping followed the loss of their cities and their best agricultural lands. The raisin cakes they had been famous for would no longer provide them their chief means of livelihood. All their pride and arrogancy would be replaced with tears. Gone were all sounds of happiness and joy. Isaiah cried out in pity for them. God's heart ached for Moab, because she was part of His family, the family of Abraham, but she had rejected God to worship at her shrines and high places. All their wearisome worship of the pagan god Chemosh had been in vain. Within three years, she would cease as a nation, and her survivors would be very few and feeble. The Moabite refugees who came to Jerusalem were to be kindly cared for. In all of these dirge poems, or songs of grief, Isaiah combines relief at the obliteration of an enemy with heartfelt sadness.

Isaiah then directs his message in Chapter 17 against Syria and Israel, because they had been united in a common attack against Judah. Thus, they were to suffer a common fate. Damascus had already been destroyed, and her people taken into captivity. Many captives had already been taken from Israel, and more were to follow. Assyria was gaining territory year by year. Almost nobody was to be spared.

Isaiah again mentions a remnant, as prophesied by the name of his first son Shear-Jashub ("The remnant shall return"). The remnant is the group that survives a time of war that is visited upon Judah because of its transgressions. The remnant is those who trust in God. The faithful in Israel escaped the Assyrian captivity by immigrating south to Judah. The coming conflict would cause the earnest and sincere to lift up their eyes to God.

Chapters 18 to 20 are focused on his prophecy about Egypt and Ethiopia (Cush). Ethiopia ruled Egypt from 715 to 663 BC during Isaiah's time. Some in Judea placed their trust in men and horses rather than in God. They thought Ethiopia and Egypt would protect them. Isaiah advised the two countries that they would gain nothing from a proposed alliance. All people were to learn that, even though it may not seem as if God is in control, His purposes will all be accomplished in the end. He directs the nations in what they can and cannot do. Nothing can happen without His knowledge. No judgment can fall without His permission. The final outcome would be a new nation that recognized the Lord.

Here is given an accurate description of the sort of debacle that so frequently meant defeat for the Egyptians. Their natural defenses were ideal, but internal unrest and dissension led to weakness and ruin. The result of their internal fighting was, at the least, chaos and anarchy and, sometimes, conquest by a foreign foe. For many centuries, Egypt would fall under the control of other nations—first Assyria, then Babylon, Persia, Macedonia, Rome, and Arabia. Their troubles came not from God, but from their refusal to walk in His ways.[20]

Then, from chapter 19, verse 18, to the end of the chapter, Isaiah presented a conditional prophecy of the time when, according to God's original plan for the evangelization of the world, the Egyptians and even the Assyrians should come to a knowledge of the true God and serve Him along with the Hebrews. The five cities mentioned may represent specific cities, or they may mean that many people would turn to the Lord and learn His ways. They would swear an oath to Him. The prophecy has not yet been fulfilled, partly because Israel

---

20 *Seventh-day Adventist Bible Commentary, Volume 4: Isaiah to Malachi* (Washington, DC: Review and Herald Publishing Association, 1955), pp. 182–183.

proved unfaithful to the sacred trust committed to her. God only allows judgments in order to restore and heal. He had good plans. He would have liked to bring salvation to all these nations, not just Judah. He is the God of all the earth and desires all nations to be saved.

Chapter 20 relates the brief story of the Assyrian King Sargon II capture of the Philistine city of Ashdod in 711 B.C. It is right on the road to Egypt. Apparently Ashdod had thought Egypt would come and help them. God used Isaiah and that event in a most unexpected way. The snippet of a story goes with the strange command that God gave. He told Isaiah to take off his outer garment and sandals as a prophecy that Egypt and Ethiopia would not be able to help anyone resist the power of Assyria. To go without the outer garment was a sign of humiliation, deprivation, and shame. For an aristocratic man like Isaiah who had always worn elegant clothes, this must have been a difficult requirement. But he had dedicated his life to fulfilling the tasks God gave him, and so he did not complain. He saw that God would use this sign to keep the coming humiliation of Egypt before the people. The leaders in Jerusalem were frequently tempted to think that Egypt and Ethiopia could protect them. God was trying to get Judah to rely on Him instead of on humans who could not help or save them. It would be three years before God would tell Isaiah he could stop walking around barefoot and put on his regular clothes again.

King Sargon II was not known outside the Bible record until the French archeologist Botta excavated Khorsabad from 1843–1845. There he uncovered the palace of Sargon II and its famous inscription of his history. He was the king who brought the Assyrian empire to its greatest height politically and militarily.

Isaiah is like one of us telling about experiences we have lived through. All his references are to historical events. But unlike us, as a prophet from God, he also received background information and predictions of the future.

In Chapter 21, Isaiah then received a vision that Babylon would fall. It was a very difficult vision for Isaiah to receive. The words he uses show how much he was affected by this vision: distress, pain, pangs of labor, bewilderment, dismay, trembling, fearfulness, and fear. His heart was broken as he realized that his people would be captives in Babylon and forced to experience what he was writing about. Elam and Media who will cooperate in bringing down Babylon are mentioned. Belshazzar's feast is also mentioned. Babylon was conquered while the king and his officials feasted on the night of the full moon. Undoubtedly, they were worshiping the moon goddess. "The carved images of her gods" (Isa. 21:9, ESV) draw attention to Babylon's idolatry.

Isaiah's attention turns to Edom, the land of Esau, southeast of Judah. Apparently, they recognized Isaiah as a prophet and send word to him to know whether he had received a prophecy for their territory. His brief response was that "the morning comes, and also the night." Maybe they would have a peaceful break before Assyria overran them entirely.

Also, representatives from the Arabian desert who were descendants of Ishmael came and asked Isaiah what news he had of their land. His answer was not hopeful. The Dedanite traders in their caravans of camels are pictured. The people of Tema are mentioned (Isa. 21:13–14). That city would be captured by Belshazzar's father Nabonidus who would kill all the inhabitants. He wanted to make Tema his headquarters for moon worship. He was born in Haran where his father was king and his mother was the high priestess of the moon goddess. Then Nebuchadnezzar conquered the area, killed his father and married his mother, so he grew up in the palace in Babylon. He married one of Nebuchadnezzar's daughters and became the last king of Babylon. He preferred to spend his time in Tema, so he made his son Belshazzar co-ruler with him and left Babylon for ten years until the Medo-Persians came to conquer Babylon. The longer details of this interesting story will have to be saved for another time.

In chapter 22, Isaiah takes a time out from prophesying about other nations to again point out serious problems in Jerusalem itself. When the people of the city should have been praying to God for help and guidance, instead they were engaged in feasting and revelry. They were also talking about which houses to tear down in order to make the wall more secure. This may have been when the Assyrian army temporarily withdrew. They probably had heard that God predicted the Assyrians would not conquer Jerusalem, but they were forgetting the suffering going on in towns all around them. It was not appropriate to celebrate when others were going through terrible circumstances. In addition, they were ignoring God Who made all things and planned for their good long ago. They should have been depending on Him, thanking Him for current blessings, and asking for His guidance for future crises that would definitely come, as well as how to help the towns around them. When they should have been weeping and wailing and tearing their hair and wearing sackcloth, instead, fatalistically, they were joyfully feasting and laughing as they said: "Let us eat and drink, for tomorrow we die" (Isa. 22:12–13).

King Hezekiah promoted weapons production, strengthened the wall, and improved the water system, but nowhere does God rebuke him for that. So, the problem here must have been the attitude of the people who were thinking only of themselves and their own good. They should have been doing whatever they could to help the towns around them, or at least been sympathetic enough to be mourning and praying for their fellow citizens. Much of their leadership had fled to some other place that they thought was safer. Obviously, many of them doubted that God would actually save them. Meanwhile, God Himself was weeping over the destruction of His people. He knew that just such a day of destruction and terror would eventually come to Jerusalem also. He warned them that these sins would not be forgiven if they died before they repented (Isa. 22:14).

> God Himself was weeping over the destruction of His people. He knew that just such a day of destruction and terror would eventually come to Jerusalem also.

Isaiah now speaks about a particularly shocking example of greed and pride. Shebna, a steward, was in charge of the palace. He was well known for his fancy chariots. He was making an impressive gravesite for himself. It was being carved out of solid rock up on a high and prominent spot. God proclaimed that he would lose his job and be sent away. There he would die, and that would be the end of his chariots and his pride (Isa 22:15-19). Eliakim, son of Hilkiah, was to take his place and receive his robes and authority. As long as Eliakim faithfully fulfilled his responsibility, he would be an honor to his family. But, if not, he could also face disgrace. God does not approve of, or support, corruption in high places. The Bible does not tell the end of the story about Shebna—not where he was exiled to or how he died—but no doubt he was not buried in his extravagant new tomb.

Chapter 23 tells the future of Tyre and Sidon, two ancient seaport cities on the Mediterranean Sea north of Judah. Both were part of Phoenicia, a nation of great seafaring builders and traders. Among other places, these nations built Carthage on the North African coast and Tarshish in Spain—where the prophet Jonah tried to flee when God told him to take a message to Ninevah. They controlled much of the trade between Egypt and other ports on the Mediterranean. As a consequence, they succumbed to pride. Here, Isaiah prophesied that they would be crushed by one superpower after another. Although they would rise again to be traders, they would continue to be harassed. This chapter says that the Assyrians had turned Babylon into a ruin, so this must have been when the city of Babylon was destroyed by Sennacherib during Isaiah's time. A few years later, Babylon was rebuilt by his son, Esarhaddon, and it would survive for many years before finally becoming a permanent ruin.

You will find summaries of the rest of the chapters in the book of Isaiah in "An Outline of Isaiah" at the end of this book.

Chapter Ten:
Gathering Clouds

In addition to all of King Hezekiah's spiritual achievements for the kingdom of Judah, he made huge defensive advances in preparation for the war with Assyria which was undoubtedly coming. All around Jerusalem, other countries were being conquered and the citizens relocated in permanent exile to other parts of the Assyrian empire. The northern kingdom of Israel had been nonexistent for a few years. Over the next seven years, the cities of Judah fell one by one. In the face of such military might, King Hezekiah did all he could to protect Jerusalem. He increased the size of the City of David by building a new wall that made the city area about four times larger. He constructed another wall outside the first one. He also removed the wall around Solomon's temple, added a new larger platform, and then built a stronger wall.

King Hezekiah's sickness, recovery, and miraculous sign happened somewhat before the crisis with Assyria. Isaiah wrote about these two events in an order that was reversed. The first half of the book of Isaiah relates to the coming Assyrian invasion. From chapter 40 to the end of the book God through Isaiah is preparing His people for the coming Babylonian captivity. Because King Hezekiah's sickness brings Babylon into the picture, Isaiah chose to tell that story after the Assyrian one.

Because King Hezekiah believed the promises given by Isaiah that Jerusalem would not be taken by Assyria, he rebelled against the king of Assyria and refused to continue sending him tribute. In order to further strengthen Judah, he defeated the Philistines all the way down to Gaza on the Mediterranean

Sea. Although the Bible does not specifically condemn him for this, he did ask Egypt for help instead of wholly trusting in God.

Jerusalem's main water supply was the Gihon Spring, which was accessible from inside the city, but its overflow watered the crops and vineyard and orchards in the Kidron Valley as well as just outside the city walls. King Hezekiah was not willing to provide good water to the Assyrian army if they attacked the city. When he put out a call for help, many people responded, and together they blocked off all the outlets where water flowed toward the Kidron Valley. But more needed to be done to protect the water and make it more accessible to the people inside the walls of Jerusalem.

An ingenious plan was devised in which two groups of men started digging a tunnel. The upper group started from the Gihon Spring. The lower group started from the Pool of Siloam, not far from the lower right corner of the city, but well away from that section of the wall. With pickaxes, the two groups hewed through the bedrock beneath the city, heading toward each other. People on the ground above them probably made noise by hitting the rocks to help them continue in the right directions. Somehow, they knew how far underground they were, and they managed to keep the tunnel sloping downhill so the water flowed and didn't pool along the way. According to the inscription they placed on the wall, when they only had four or five feet to go, they could hear each other's voices, and they quickly used their pickaxes to break through. From one end of the 1750-foot tunnel to the other, there was only a difference of twelve inches in the level of the stone floor! It was an amazing engineering feat.[21]

King Hezekiah also led the people in preparing armaments for war. He had large numbers of weapons and shields made. He appointed military officers over the people, assembled them before him in the square at the city gate, and gave them an inspirational message. "Be strong and courageous. Do not be afraid or discouraged because of the king of Assyria and the vast army with him, for there is a greater power with us than with him. With him is only the arm of flesh, but with us is the Lord our God to help us and to fight our battles." His speech greatly encouraged the people. Because of his faith in God's word, the people had greater faith that what God had promised would actually happen.

It had now been twenty-two years since Samaria was overrun. Meanwhile the Assyrian army continued attacking one town after another. Finally, they were besieging Lachish, a town only thirty-nine miles southwest of Jerusalem. It was the second most important city in Judah. The two cities could send signals and information to each other from the tops of nearby hills. By now, it was obvious to all who had read the message, that Isaiah had, years before, accurately predicted what would happen to Jerusalem. It was now standing alone like a little hut in the middle of a melon field. All the other towns had been attacked and conquered. In fact, King Sennacherib claimed to have shut King Hezekiah up like a bird in a cage and to have taken lots of captives from Judah that year. If we can believe what he said, he claimed to have taken daughters of the royal household, royal concubines, and male and female musicians. Undoubtedly many of Judah's bravest soldiers were killed, and probably many others were taken captive. Jerusalem was in danger so extreme that it was not humanly possible the people could escape being conquered by the Assyrian army.

Even Hezekiah's faith may have wavered. He sent a message to the king of Assyria in Lachish: "I have done wrong. Withdraw from me, and I will pay whatever you demand of me" (2 Kings 18:14).

Soon the answer came back. The king of Assyria demanded three hundred talents of silver and thirty talents of gold. A talent was at least thirty-three

---

21   I encourage you to watch "The Story of Hezekiah's Tunnel" on YouTube. It is very graphic and interesting.

kilograms or 72.75 pounds. Quickly King Hezekiah sent him all the silver that was found in the temple of the Lord and in the treasuries of the royal palace. Then he stripped off the gold with which he had covered the doors and doorposts of the temple of the Lord and sent that also to the king of Assyria. Hezekiah and others in the kingdom must have been hopeful that this would make Assyria leave Jerusalem alone. Maybe, they thought, this was how God would fulfill His promise to protect them.

Chapter Eleven:
The Storm Breaks

The pay-off was not to bring the result that King Hezekiah wanted. A massive Assyrian army marched in and set up camp outside the gates of Jerusalem. Other portions of the army were guarding the road on the Mediterranean coast, the only way from the south where the Egyptian army could have come to Jerusalem's aid. The Assyrian king and more troops yet were completing the conquest of Lachish, the second most important city in Judah. The two cities were close enough to each other that signals sent from the tops of hills could be seen between the towns, so it was well known that Lachish soon would be completely destroyed. Now all possible help had been cut off. In this ominous state of affairs, the people of Jerusalem held their breath and waited. Many watched from the walls to see what would happen next. Before long, a deputation of three men approached the city gate.

They called for King Hezekiah. He sent three men down to talk to them. One of them was Shebna, the secretary who liked chariots, but he no longer had his previously high position. By this time, Eliakim was the palace administrator, and his name meant "God will establish." The message delivered to them by the Assyrian commander was this: "On what are you basing this confidence of yours? On whom are you depending, that you rebel against me? Look now, you are depending on Egypt, that splintered reed of a staff which pierces a man's hand and wounds him if he leans on it! And if you say to me, 'We are depending on the Lord our God'—isn't He the one whose high places and altars Hezekiah removed?'"

Obviously, this man was no expert on the pagan gods versus the God of Judah.

The message continued: "Furthermore, have I come to attack and destroy this place without word from the Lord? The Lord himself told me to march against this country and destroy it.

By this time, the delegation sent by King Hezekiah was becoming distraught. They pleaded with the Assyrian to speak in Aramaic which they knew, rather than in the Hebrew language which all the people on the wall could hear and understand.

The arrogant reply came swiftly. "Was it only to your master and you that my master sent me to say these things, and not to the men sitting on the wall—who, like you, will have to eat their own filth and drink their own urine?" That unfortunate speech revealed how terrible it was to have the Assyrian army besieging a city!

Then the commander raised his voice and yelled so that all the people could clearly hear him. "Don't let King Hezekiah deceive you. He cannot deliver you from my hand. Do not let him persuade you to trust in the Lord when he says, 'The Lord will surely deliver us.'

"Do not listen to Hezekiah. The king of Assyria invites you to make peace with him. Then you will have time to eat and drink on your own property before he takes you into a good land like your own." In other words, the people of Jerusalem would maybe have a little space of time on their farms before he exiled them (forever) to other parts of his empire. The commander continued to blaspheme and belittle the Creator God, whom he said could not possibly save them from Assyria. Humanly speaking, he was telling the truth.

All the people remained silent and did not say a word, because that was what Hezekiah had told them to do. His three representatives returned to the king with their clothes torn to show how upset they were. When they delivered the message, King Hezekiah also tore his clothes and put on sackcloth as well, to show how horrified and concerned he was. He went into the temple and sent the men with a message for the prophet Isaiah. He told them to say. "This is a day of distress and rebuke and disgrace. It may be that the Lord your God will hear all the words of the field commander, whom his master, the king of Assyria, has sent to ridicule the living God, and that He will rebuke him for the words the Lord your God has heard. Please pray for us!"

Back came this message from Isaiah: "Tell your master, 'This is what the Lord says: Do not be afraid of what you have heard—those words with which the underlings of the king of Assyria have blasphemed Me. Listen! I am going to put such a spirit in him that when he hears a certain report, he will return to his own country, and there he will be cut down with the sword.'"

Before long, the commander heard that the king of Assyria had left Lachish. Accordingly, he left behind the massive army that had accompanied him to Jerusalem. He found the king fighting a few miles north against the town of Libnah. Shortly after that, the king received a report that the Ethiopian king of Egypt was marching out to fight him, so he sent another threatening, blasphemous letter to King Hezekiah. Then King Sennacherib left the area to fight against the Egyptians.

From historical sources, we find that the entire Assyrian army withdrew from Jerusalem at that time, but they returned a couple of years later. The second time the King of Assyria and probably his whole army were gathered there. They had conquered all the other surrounding towns and nations. History does not report that Jerusalem alone had held out against them. That has to be inferred from the Bible story. Assyrian sources give details about Lachish and other places, but they don't tell us what happened in Jerusalem. Ancient nations never reported on their failures, only their victories.

When King Hezekiah received the latest message, he read it, then went up to the temple and spread the message out before the Lord and prayed, finishing with this: "Now O Lord our God, deliver us from his hand, so that all kingdoms on earth may know that you alone, O Lord, are God."

The prophet Isaiah soon sent a message to Hezekiah. "This is what the Lord, the God of Israel says: 'I have heard your prayer concerning Sennacherib king of Assyria. This is the word that the Lord has spoken against him:

'Who is it you have ridiculed and blasphemed?

'Against whom have you raised your voice and lifted your eyes in pride?
'Against the Holy One of Israel!
'By your messengers you have heaped insults on the Lord.
'You have bragged about all kinds of things you have done.
'Have you not heard that long ago I permitted, planned, and brought to pass those very things you are bragging about?
'You have only destroyed and scorched parts of the earth because I allowed it.
'But I know where you stay and when you come and go and how you rage against Me.
"Because your insolence has reached My ears, I will put My hook in your nose and My bit in your mouth,
'And I will make you return by the way you came.'"

Isaiah also had words of comfort and promise for King Hezekiah. He could go home and sleep well that night. The succeeding order and timing of events is uncertain. In the Bible, these occurred the next morning. History makes us think it might have been later when the Assyrian king and his army returned.

Either way, one morning there was incredible news: The entire Assyrian army lay dead outside the walls of Jerusalem. It only took one angel to put the whole army to sleep permanently. That report was the one God had said would cause King Sennacherib to break camp and return to Nineveh and stay there. His army was now so small that, as God had predicted, a child could count the soldiers.

While King Sennacherib was worshiping one day in the temple of his god Nisroch, two of his sons killed him with a sword. They escaped to the land of Ararat, and Esarhaddon, another of his sons, succeeded Sennacherib as king.

Meanwhile, back in Jerusalem, whatever the Assyrian soldiers had been carrying with them was free for the taking. There must have been stacks of plunder. But imagine the huge task of disposing of all those bodies before they began to decompose and stink. Maybe there were hundreds of fires to help do the job. The whole population of Judah must have turned out to help.

I am sure, as compassionate as God is, He sorrowed for all those Assyrian young men. Like the guards who threw Daniel's three friends into the furnace on the Plain of Dura, they were collateral damage. How much God would have preferred to save them and enjoy eternal life with them. Unfortunately, they were in a situation that removed them from the protection and blessings He would have loved to pour out on them. However, if there were some of them who would have chosen to love and worship Him, God knew their hearts, and they will be raised in the first resurrection to live forever with God's family.

* * * * *

Isaiah's prophecies in the first thirty-seven chapters mainly focus on preparing the people of Judah to withstand the Assyrian invasion. The annihilation of the Assyrian army was a mighty miracle on the order of the Exodus and crossing the Red Sea and crossing the Jordan on dry land when they entered the Promised Land. It drew Judah back to God and renewed their faith in His ability and willingness to save them.

Then, with danger from the Assyrians mostly behind them, Isaiah's focus shifted to the even-worse calamity that was coming a century later. The tone of the rest of his book is completely different. If Jerusalem had been conquered by Assyria, all the people would have been permanently scattered throughout the vast Assyrian empire. They would have blended in with the societies around them and lost their Jewish identity, as happened to the ten tribes of the northern kingdom. There would not have been a homeland for the promised Messiah.

> *I am sure, as compassionate as God is, He sorrowed for all those Assyrian young men. How much God would have preferred to save them and enjoy eternal life with them. However, if there were some of them who would have chosen to love and worship Him, God knew their hearts, and they will be raised in the first resurrection to live forever with God's family.*

When Babylon showed up at the walls of Jerusalem, God did not perform a miracle to deliver the city. Because of the people's ongoing idolatry, they would be taken captive to Babylon for seventy years. As Isaiah's first son's name predicted, (Shear-Jashub), a remnant would return at the end of that time. And as his second son's name predicted, (Maher-Shalal-Hash-Baz), that time would undoubtedly come. Throughout that long century until the captivity, and then through the seventy years' wait to return home, God's people would need comfort and assurance that God had not abandoned them. Isaiah finishes his prophecy by bidding them look in faith at the glorious prospect after their return from captivity. He focused on the righteousness of God and majored in the promises of the outpouring of God's grace upon the righteous.

PART V:

Manasseh, the King

Chapter Twelve:
Wait on the Lord[22]

Eventually the same thing happened to good King Hezekiah that happens to everyone else. He died. He must have been counting down those extra fifteen years and knew when his time was coming to a close. "So, Hezekiah rested with his fathers, and they buried him in the upper tombs of the sons of David; and all Judah and the inhabitants of Jerusalem honored him at his death."

It turned out as well as possible. Everyone in the nation and the city honored him. And it sounds as though he was buried in a very exclusive place. Everyone from God to the prophet Isaiah and on down to all the citizens of Judah and Jerusalem agreed that he was a good king.

And yet the next sentence in his obituary is ominous. "Then Manasseh his son reigned in his place." He became co-ruler with Hezekiah when he was twelve years old. For nine years, until his father died, they ruled together. That means Manasseh was six years old when his father had the boil and would have died, but God gave Hezekiah fifteen more years of life. It is interesting to think about what might have happened if Manasseh had become the sole king when he was six years old. But he didn't, and the Bible doesn't tell us any more about it.

When he was twelve and was named the co-ruler, he was almost a teenager. Maybe he became rebellious the next year and thought he knew better than his father. Of course, he was only the co-ruler, and his father could still tell him what to do. That may have annoyed him, seeing as how he knew so

---

[22] The stories of King Manasseh are found in 2 Kings 21:1–18; 2 Chronicles 33:1–20.

much better, and all. Maybe he went from one exasperation to another for the final years of his father's life, refusing to learn anything about the proper way to govern a nation that claimed to serve the God of heaven. Undoubtedly there were bad influences around him that were eager to see Judah go back to worshiping idols. Well, they had found their man. I hope King Hezekiah died without knowing too much about this. It would have broken his heart. By the time Manasseh became sole ruler, he was in his very early twenties, probably not quite mature enough to have figured out that his father had tried to do what was right. By this time, Isaiah had been a prophet for at least sixty years. He had worked closely with these kings—Uzziah, Jotham, even wicked Ahaz, and then good Hezekiah. In his work as court historian in the palace, he knew all the ins and outs of each reign. Since he was related to all of them, he had free access to the royal family. He and Yishka had great grandchildren. His mother Anyah had long since died. His sons were still evidence that God was controlling the destiny of Judah. Their first son, Shear-Jashub, was named the promise: "A remnant shall return." The second son, Maher-Shalal-Hash-Baz, was the warning of what the future would hold: "Quick to the plunder, swift to the spoil."

Deborah and her family visited them regularly. Her son, Immanuel, had had a good position in the palace for years, and his name was still a reminder that "God is with us." Now that his uncle Hezekiah had died, he was waiting to see whether his cousin Manasseh would want him to continue in the same position.

One day Deborah came to see Isaiah. She told him that she was seeing the priests who used to be in the temple of Baal and the temple of Moloch. It had been years, but now they were appearing in the palace to talk with King Manasseh. And they had younger men with them. Isaiah warned her that she and Immanuel with his family needed to get away from the palace. If the idolatrous priests came back into power, they would definitely recognize her and want to eliminate her and her son. Fortunately, Immanuel had years ago been able to get back the property his father's family had lost. A caretaker was maintaining it for him. Now they were able to quickly move back to the farm which was far from Jerusalem and isolated even from small towns. It was a culture shock to adjust to farm life, but they were soon very glad they had moved there. Shear-Jashub helped them move so he would know where they resided. That way, if things got really bad, Isaiah and his extended family could join them there.

It wasn't long before all of them knew just how bad things were becoming. King Manasseh, the sole ruler, took the advice of the idolatrous priests and reestablished the detestable practices of the nations the Lord had driven out of the land. The king rebuilt the high places his father had demolished; he also erected altars to the Baals and made Asherah poles. He bowed down to all the starry hosts and worshiped them. In both courts of the temple of the Lord, he built altars to the sun, moon, and stars. He sacrificed his sons in the fire in the Valley of Ben Hinnom; practiced sorcery, divination, and witchcraft; and consulted mediums and spiritists. He took the carved image he had made and put it in God's temple. King Manasseh led Judah and the people of Jerusalem astray, so they did more evil than the Canaanites who had lived in the land before the Israelites.

As usual, Isaiah boldly spoke whatever the Lord told him. He had always been respected and listened to. Throughout his sixty years as a prophet, even though many of his messages had been hard on sinners' ears, nobody had ever questioned his right or duty to deliver the words God wanted people to hear. When God gave him another message (you can read this in Isaiah 65:1–16), he didn't hesitate to deliver it. It is clear that sinners in Israel will not be counted as children of Abraham. The righteous in every part of the world are true servants of God. It is a stern message of warning that life for the sinners will be very different from life for those who choose God's way. He wrote out the message and went to the temple to read it to the assembled worshipers. Then he read a second message God had given him specifically for King Manasseh.

> *The righteous in every part of the world are true servants of God.*

"Manasseh king of Judah has committed these detestable sins. He has done more evil than the Amorites who preceded him and has led Judah into sin with his idols. Therefore, this is what the Lord, the God of Israel says: I am going to bring such disaster on Jerusalem and Judah, that the ears of everyone who hears of it will tingle. I will stretch out over Jerusalem the measuring line used against Samaria and the plumb line used against the house of Ahab; I will wipe out Jerusalem as one wipes a dish, wiping it and turning it upside down. I will forsake the remnant of my inheritance and give them into the hand of enemies. They will be looted and plundered by all their enemies; they have done evil in My eyes and have aroused My anger from the day their ancestors came out of Egypt until this day" (2 Kings 21:11–15).

Spies were there who immediately took a report back to King Manasseh. He was highly incensed. This was too much. Isaiah had crossed the line. And he, Manasseh, was the king! He could do whatever he wanted. He had Isaiah arrested and stuffed into a hollow log. Then servants were instructed to cut the log in half.[23] The shock for Isaiah's family was beyond description. Yishka had a heart attack and died the same day. Immediately after burying their parents, the two boys talked to their sisters and brothers-in-law, inviting them to flee with them. Those who chose to go left secretly for Immanuel's farm.

They escaped none too soon. King Manasseh and his cohorts decided to clear the city of those who insisted on worshiping God and criticizing anyone who did not. So much blood was shed that it filled Jerusalem from one end to the other. Surely, you would think, God would get rid of Manasseh and find another better king. But no, God knew something no one could know. Manasseh reigned longer than any other king of Judah, fifty-five years.

To those who wait on the Lord, restoration and renewal are sure to come. Isaiah had written that the concept of waiting on the Lord distinguishes God's faithful people from those who do not trust Him and instead take things into their own hands. The righteous people who lived in the land after Isaiah was killed had to wait years to see what God would do for their kingdom.

Assyria had regained some of its former power. After many years of King Manasseh's reign, army commanders of the king of Assyria took Manasseh prisoner, put a hook in his nose, bound him with bronze shackles and took him to Babylon. Remember, that was a seventeen-hundred-mile journey. Maybe the soldiers were pulling him along by the hook in his nose. Ouch! It would have been a miserable trip, and it gave him a lot of time to think. Probably he remembered what Isaiah had said would happen to him. Probably he also had some good memories of his father. He must have ended up with a terribly guilty conscience.

In his distress he sought the favor of the Lord his God and humbled himself greatly before the God of his fathers. And when he prayed to Him, the Lord was moved by his entreaty and listened to his plea. Amazingly, he was able to return to Jerusalem and to his kingdom. Then King Manasseh knew that the Lord is God. The rest of his life he tried to undo all the damage he had done. It was much harder to persuade everyone else to worship God, than it had been to lead them into worshiping idols. The consequences for Jerusalem remained. King Manasseh's grandson would be the only other good king. Not many years later, Judah would go into the seventy-year captivity to Babylon. As God had promised, a remnant would return to rebuild Jerusalem. In the fulness of time, the Messiah—so perfectly described by Isaiah—would come and show what God is like. After thirty-three years, He would die for all of us and ultimately save the universe from the poison of sin.

---

23   See Hebrews 11:37.

Because he finally repented and humbled himself before God, King Manasseh himself will be resurrected to spend eternity with God—and with Isaiah. Can you imagine how surprised Isaiah will be? When he hears the whole story, I'm sure he will be thrilled that God's grace was sufficient even for Manasseh. Yishka will also end up happy that God is so merciful and forgiving that there is no sin He is not eager to cover, if the sinner will just repent and turn to God, humbly pleading for another chance to live in harmony with Him. God is not willing that any should perish.

Don't let anything steal your chance of being there with Isaiah and Yishka and all the saved, especially with your elder Brother Jesus, our Savior!

An Outline of Isaiah

Chapters 1–5: Word pictures of idolatry and evil among God's people, and the results of their bad choices versus God's good plans for them and His great desire to restore righteousness and peace among them. There is a huge contrast between the end result for the righteous and the end result for the wicked.

Chapter 6: Isaiah's vision of God and his call to be a prophet.

Chapters 7–12: The Immanuel Volume. The soon-to-come human baby and the ultimate promised Son, called Wonderful, Counselor, Everlasting Father, Mighty God, Prince of Peace, the Branch, the Root of Jesse—all titles of reassurance that God is with us and He will finally restore the earth to perfection for all creation.

Chapters 13–23: God reveals to Israel the condition and future of all the surrounding nations. Each of them is a seeming threat to the continuation of the kingdom of Judah, but God is in control of what will actually take place. Even Jerusalem is included in the oracles because her unfaithfulness is in danger of bringing upon God's people the consequences of not trusting in Him. Chapter 14 includes the first clear picture in the Bible of the background story to the serpent in Eden.

Chapters 24–27: Isaiah's Apocalypse, so named because of its broad scope, taking in the whole world. Here for the first time in the Bible is found the millennium, the desolation of the earth, the forces of evil shut up in a dungeon to be loosed after many days, the end of death, the resurrection and salvation of the righteous, and the final end of the wicked. In beautiful language, Isaiah assures us that the Lord "will swallow up death forever and the Lord God will wipe away tears from all faces." (Isa. 25:8)

These chapters also have wonderful promises for the righteous, even some of the most memorable in the Bible. Read Isaiah. 25:9 and Isaiah. 26:3, 19. My favorite is Isaiah. 26:12 (NIV). As you read about destruction and judgment, it is well to remember that, in the Old Testament, God is blamed for everything that happens. Certainly, nothing is done without His permission, but we need to be careful to remember that God is love, He is not arbitrary, and He does not use force. If we take into consideration the whole Bible, we find that there is someone else who is to blame for the terrible things that happen.

Chapters 28–33: Six woe messages give warnings alternating with promises of salvation. The promises contain some of the most remarkable designations of God. The Lord is introduced as a Savior, a crown of glory and a diadem of beauty for the remnant of His people, a cornerstone which is a sure foundation, a teacher, the Lord of hosts wonderful in counsel and excellent in guidance.

Chapter 28: First Woe to Ephraim (another name for Israel, the northern kingdom). The alternative to a covenant with God is a covenant with death. God's unusual act, or God's strange act, is to use foreign nations to execute judgment upon His people. Choosing God is choosing life. Like a good father, God does everything in the right way and at the right time. Listen to His teaching and trust Him with your life.

Chapter 29: Second Woe to Jerusalem. The paradox is a place called city of God (Ariel) where people turn away from God. They continue all the rituals and sacrifices while their hearts are far from Him. The promise is that in the future they will turn back to God, the Holy One of Israel.

Chapter 30: Third Woe to the rebellious children. When there was fear of Israel and Syria, the king of Judah put his trust in Assyria. When it became clear who the real enemy was, then Judah put its trust in Egypt. Meanwhile, God was eagerly waiting to show mercy and compassion on His people. He wants to heal His people and bind up their wounds.

Chapters 31–32: Fourth Woe to those who go down to Egypt for help. They just cannot seem to learn how foolish it is to not trust God and wait on

An Outline of Isaiah

Him for help. God would fight for them as He did for the children of Israel when they left Egypt. A righteous king is coming.

Chapter 33: Fifth Woe to you who plunder though you have not been plundered; and you who deal treacherously, though they have not dealt treacherously with you. Sinners will be totally consumed by fire. The righteous will see the King in His beauty. Then continues a list of things they will see and things they will not see.

Chapter 34: Sixth Woe to all nations, people, the earth, and world. Isaiah's language depicts end-time events.

Chapter 35: A vision of the joy of salvation. This will be the new reality of God's kingdom: joy and gladness instead of sorrow and sighing. The ultimate fulfillment of the prophecies of this chapter will occur at the second coming of Christ and on the new earth.

Chapters 36–37: In an historical interlude, Isaiah mostly abandons poetry for prose to tell about the Assyrian invasion. Sennacherib boasts that God cannot deliver Jerusalem, Isaiah assures the king of deliverance, Hezekiah prays, Isaiah reports what the Lord has to say about Sennacherib, then God sends one lone angel who puts to sleep forever the Assyrian troops. An amazing deliverance! Like during the Exodus and in Gideon's war with the Midianites, God's people did not have to fight. God totally took care of the problem.

Chapters 38–39: In a second story (which actually happened before the Assyrians besieged Jerusalem), King Hezekiah is dying from the infection of a boil. God sent the prophet Isaiah to tell him to set his house in order. The king wept bitterly and prayed for God to remember all the good he had done and to let him live longer. Isaiah was sent back with a positive response including a remedy and a sign, which led to the biggest mistake Hezekiah ever made.

Chapter 40: This chapter begins with "Comfort, comfort my people," and sounds as though the Babylonian captivity is already a thing of the past. The rest of the chapter emphasizes the power and sovereignty of God. The nations cannot be an obstacle to God's plan. There is a simple reason why God chose to speak as though the danger from Babylon was past.

In Bible times, people liked to know what was going to happen before they heard what events lead up to it. In other words, they liked to read the end of the book before they read the book. That is called *thinking from effect to cause*. Nowadays we tend to reason from cause to effect, waiting until the end of the story to find out what finally happens. Here in chapter 40, we find the end of the story, the effect-to-cause reasoning that people preferred in Isaiah's day. God comforts His people, the war is over, iniquity is removed, the time of judgment has expired, the end of the exile has come, the new exodus back to Jerusalem can occur, the revelation of God's glory is available to contemplate, the time of fear is passed, and God's reign has arrived. Now that the conclusion of the story has been told, Isaiah will continue with the rest of the divine revelations he receives from God to help those of Judah prepare for the coming events which will not be easy ones.

Chapter 41: One of the most interesting predictions in Isaiah is about Cyrus. He would be born a century later in Medo-Persia. God planned a special work for him, and even called him "shepherd" and "anointed," the same words that in other places refer to Jesus Christ. Cyrus would be another savior, because he would allow the people of Judah to go back to Jerusalem at the end of 70 years. In chapter 41:2, God asks the question, "Who has stirred up one from the east, calling him in righteousness to his service?" Toward the end of the chapter, in verse 25, God again speaks of Cyrus. "I have stirred up one from the north, and he comes—one from the rising sun who calls on My name." He would come from the east as well as from the north.

Once Egypt in the south had lost its power, all the succeeding conquerors had to come from the north. It was the only possible route. The desert to the east was too barren and dry to support an army trying to cross it. So the army from Babylon, and later Medo-Persia, had to follow the Tigris and Euphrates river to the north until they reached Haran where Abraham had lived. Then they could come south to attack God's people in Jerusalem. Later, Greek and Roman armies travelled toward the east until they could come south toward Jerusalem. So after Egypt, all other conquering armies came from the north. This is why they are referred to in other places as the king of the North.

History proved God's predictions to be exactly right. A whole book could be written about Cyrus' various conquests that are briefly described by Isaiah. The one big example is that after he conquered Babylon, he let the Judean captives go home. No gods could begin to compare with Jehovah God's ability to foretell the future.

An Outline of Isaiah

Chapter 42:1–9: is the first of four Servant Songs of Isaiah. These four "Servant Songs" describe the coming messianic King and are key to the New Testament understanding of Jesus. In chapter 42, Isaiah begins to give us a more complete picture of the Messiah and His mission to the world. God the Father would be completely pleased with Him. Jesus would receive the fullness of God's Spirit. Furthermore, He is described in ways that fit perfectly with His life on earth. Kedar is an Arabian tribe descended from Ishmael. Sela is Petra where descendants of Esau lived. Both represent distant people who would turn to God.

Chapter 43: God reveals both His plans of hope as well as His frustration over Israel. He asserts that Israel was His witness, the servant He had chosen who was to disclose to the heathen nations the true character and nature of God. But they, like the fig tree, were covered with leaves without fruit. They were as pretentious foliage. So, God says, "I will do a new thing" (verse 19). Nearly a century later, they would be sent to Babylon as fugitives to cure them of their idolatry. Then, He who had rescued them from Egypt would also rescue them from Babylon. They should not even think about the former rescue, because the coming captivity and deliverance would be "a new thing," fully as miraculous as the exodus from Egypt. The chapter ends with the comparison of the persistent unfaithfulness of Israel with the steady faithfulness of God.

Chapter 44: Here are promises about our children. In verse 2, Jeshurun means "my little Jacob." Verse 5 is a wonderful promise we can pray for our children. The same God who promises to pour out His Spirit on our offspring clearly states that there is no one like Him (verse 6) and one proof He gives is His ability to tell the future (verse 7). At the end of the chapter, He names Cyrus and foretells events connected with him.

Chapter 45: Continues about Cyrus. and the story of the conquest of Babylon, prophesied many years ahead of time. He is called "anointed" which is the translation of "Messiah." That term was applied to both the High Priest and the king. Jesus at His baptism was anointed by the Holy Spirit as the promised Messiah. Cyrus' version of the story—written on the Cyrus Cylinder, now in the British Museum—tells of the conquest of Babylon without a battle and the subsequent release of captives to worship as they saw fit in their own lands. The Greek historian, Herodotus, fills in some of the details. Cyrus' favorite horse drowned in the river Euphrates. Upset with the river, he had his men dig canals coming out of it to dry up the river. That was not a terribly hard job, since canals had been dug some time before in order to construct the bridge which crossed the river. His men just had to open the dikes to once again send the water out into the desert instead of downstream. Soon his army was able to wade through the river bed into the city through the open gates. The knowledge of God would spread widely through the influence of Cyrus. And the Jews would be cured of idolatry by their seventy years in Babylon.

Chapter 46: *Bel* means "lord." It was the title for Marduk, the national god of Babylon. Nabu, the god of knowledge and literature, was regarded as the son of Marduk. His seat of worship was at Borsippa, about 11 miles southwest of Babylon. Every New Year, Nabu was carried the eleven miles to Babylon to visit Marduk. Then Marduk accompanied Nabu part of the way back to Borsippa. Both of them would be transported on carts pulled by animals. Once, years before, Marduk was stolen as part of the spoils of war. Later, he was restored to Babylon. Which just goes to show that idols are totally helpless to protect themselves or the people who worship them. By contrast with the incompetent gods of Babylon, God Himself carries His own worshippers from birth to death! (verses 3, 4)

How hard it is for us to deal with the silence of God! Only focusing our thoughts on Him who declares "the end from the beginning" (verse 10) will bring about the assurance that His salvation "shall not linger" (verse 13). Let us daily concentrate on God and remember that His deliverance is near.

Chapter 47: With the Assyrian army destroyed by God, that danger was mostly past. Now God's people needed to know about Babylon, the kingdom that would take them into captivity. This chapter reveals what will happen to them there—but much more; it is the assurance that God is Sovereign, and Babylon will not last forever. The kingdom will be unmasked and shown to be a prostitute and slave instead of a queen. Babylon boasted of her religion, but inwardly it was an abomination. She depended on sorcery and potent spells to keep her safe. Astrology was invented in Babylon, and then exported to Egypt and other countries. By the practice of occult magic, the Babylonian sorcerers professed to be in touch with the gods. Daniel, chapters 2, 4, and 5 prove that they were not. Here Isaiah describes the fall of Babylon. God foretells its downfall a century and a half before it took place. In fact,

An Outline of Isaiah

He foretold it before the Neo-Babylonian Empire rose to prominence. Much of this chapter again appears in the book of Revelation.

Chapter 48: The wayward children of Judah are made to face the foreknowledge of God. "Oh, that you had heeded My commandments!" says God. "Then your peace would have been like a river (verse 18) Instead, "there is no peace,…for the wicked" (verse 22). In verse 16, we find the entire Godhead at work on their behalf! Four times in the chapter, God pleads with the hypocrites in Israel who profess to serve Him. He has foretold events so they could never say that their gods foretold them. Which one of their gods told them about Cyrus ahead of time? If only they had paid attention! But God was not going to allow His plans to come to naught.

Chapter 49: Here begins an important section (chapters 49–53) in which the "servant" spoken of is primarily Christ. The theme of this section is the glorious mission of God's "servant" and His ministry in this world. Israel is to be restored, and the Gentiles are to be gathered in. "Is it really possible for captives to be taken away from tyrants?" "Yes," says the Lord. "It will happen, and I will save your children. (*Children* meant descendants of the Jews.) Your oppressors will destroy themselves. Then everyone will know that I, the Lord, am your Savior, your Redeemer, the Mighty One of Jacob."

Chapter 50: God speaks to Judah in irony. He did not divorce Judah. She left Him. He tried every way possible to persuade her to return. Hosea, a prophet to Israel, the northern ten tribes, was Isaiah's contemporary. His marriage was an acted parable of what God is saying here to Judah, the southern kingdom. With verse 4, a new section is introduced with more details about Jesus, the servant. Although the plan for His life was laid out in detail before He came to earth, He laid aside His foreknowledge and communed with His Father day by day to know His will. In the future, people will come from every direction to share in the comfort

> *Although the plan for His life was laid out in detail before He came to earth, He laid aside His foreknowledge and communed with His Father day by day to know His will.*

and compassion the Lord offers to those afflicted. "Sinim" is probably China. Today, there are many thousands turning to Jesus Christ in that great country.

Verse 6 says "I offered…my cheeks to those who pulled out my beard." The same verse in the Isaiah text from the Dead Sea Scrolls and also from the Greek translation used in the first century employ the word slap instead of *pull* or *pluck*. And that is what we read happened at His crucifixion. Even at the cross, Jesus was not cowed. He knew who He was and Who had sent Him. He firmly determined to carry through the entire plan.

Chapter 51: Isaiah now addresses the devout in Israel. Three parties are in constant conversation: Isaiah, the righteous that remain in Judah, and God.

Here are two examples of double vocatives which are a sign of deep emotion and concern. When the devout of Judah appeal to God, they cry, "Awake, awake, put on strength, O arm of the Lord." Verse 9. Then in verse 17, God answers Jerusalem: "Awake, awake! Stand up, O Jerusalem." They can trust God's word because He is all powerful. Just as He can control the sea and create heaven and earth, He can care for His people. God sees what is happening. He takes note and will bring about justice for all.

Chapter 52: This chapter finishes the "Wake up" Zion sermon, then begins a new section on the suffering of the Servant. The good news is four-fold: peace, glad tidings, salvation, and confirmation that God is still on His throne. A young man is commissioned by the commander on the field of battle to run and deliver the message that the king has won. When they see him coming a watchman proclaims, "How beautiful on the mountains are the feet of him who brings good news."

Then Isaiah sees the defeat of Babylon and the triumph of God, and tells the people, "Depart! Depart! Go out from there…go out from the midst of her…" This is another call to come out of Babylon, for she represents death, and God has secured life and freedom for His people. When the Israelites left Egypt, it was an emergency to leave before pharaoh changed his mind. From the Babylonian captivity they would not have to rush. Cyrus proclaimed liberty when they still had time to pack and wait for the dry season to travel. Then they were able to make the long journey and arrive back in Jerusalem just when the seventy

An Outline of Isaiah

years of captivity were ending. Unfortunately, most of the Jews chose to stay in Babylon. They had nice lives there. Going back to Jerusalem was starting all over again, which is hard work.

From verse 13 to the end of the chapter, is an introduction to the next chapter, chapter 53. God's Servant will do with wisdom just what He came to do. He will humble Himself, veiling His divinity with humanity. Then He will be highly honored and greatly exalted by God. It will be His sacrifice that will make possible all the glorious future God has in store for His people from every part of the world.

Chapter 53 is the fourth of the "Servant Songs" in Isaiah. It is made up of five sections, three verses each.

It tells the depths of pain suffered by Jesus, as God's Servant on behalf of sinners. Jesus asked the rabbis about this at the age of twelve. This gave Him his first insight into His mission as the Substitute. This is what the Ethiopian eunuch was reading when Philip came to help him.

This chapter is about the core of Jesus' mission and His death on the cross for mankind and the whole universe. It's hard to believe it was written about 700 years before Jesus was born. Isaiah must have been astonished and amazed by this revelation. The coming Messiah was not the kind of Messiah the Jews were expecting or interested in. The vicarious nature of Christ's sufferings and death is reiterated nine times (verses 4–6, 8, 11, and 12). No wonder the book of Isaiah is called the "Fifth Gospel."

Chapter 54: God speaks affectionately to those who know Him, and the language is simply beautiful. God is our Creator, Redeemer, Husband, and Teacher. But the predominant language is of Him as our loving Husband.

Chapter 55: God directs Himself to the heathen. Water, wine, milk, and bread represent the blessings of salvation. Even though we have no money, we are urged to buy, i.e., we must be willing to part with

Salvation is free, yet its blessings may be obtained only at the cost of all that one has.

everything we hold dear in order to receive the One for whom our soul longs. It's more about letting go than about having the power to buy. The poetic beauty of this chapter is unsurpassed in Scripture. It begins with a fourfold invitation: "Come." To get the good things in life, you just have to come. Salvation is free, yet its blessings may be obtained only at the cost of all that one has. Water, wine, milk and food (literally "fatness") represent all spiritual blessings. The sinner's every need will be supplied in Christ Jesus. The chapter closes with one of Isaiah's favorite themes: the transformation of the world from a barren wilderness into a flourishing garden.

Chapter 56 is about the conversion of the Gentiles and the outcasts as compared to the leadership of Israel's unreadiness to do the task God had given them. All are to share equally in the privileges and responsibilities involved in the covenant relationship. No one, from whatever nation or with whatever handicap, should ever feel that they are outside of God's love.

The scene changes as Isaiah depicts the wretched spiritual condition of leaders and people and its results. This line of thought continues without interruption through chapter 57:12.

Chapter 57: The righteous dead escape from evil. They are resting securely in peace. Death delivers them from greater evils that would befall them were they to live on. On the other hand, the wicked are worshipping pagan symbols and living in fear and dread but are not willing to submit to God. Isaiah may be describing idolatrous conditions during the opening part of the reign of King Manasseh. These strong warnings might have been what lead to Isaiah's death/murder. For the last seven verses, God expresses His willingness to forgive and heal and welcome anyone. The gospel is the message of peace. The wicked have no possibility of peace because peace is the fruit of righteousness.

Chapter 58: God instructs Isaiah to ramp up the decibels. Maybe He is giving a hint that Isaiah's time is short. The people of Judah wonder why God isn't paying attention to them. God compares what they do when they fast with the kind of fast He wants them to observe. He wants them to show mercy and compassion for the oppressed and the hungry and the poor and the naked. If they would do that, their lives would dramatically change for the better. They would accomplish great things. Immediately the focus turns to the Sabbath, suggesting this change for the better will be part of what they will repair and rebuild. If they delight in the Lord, they will be filled with joy. God will delight in them and be able to do all for them that He wishes to do.

Chapter 59: This chapter summarizes the major issue of the book of Isaiah. Their sinful practices have erected a barrier between them and God. They admit God's charges against them. Then is seen a striking description of the results of transgression. Justice is personified and pictured as having fled away for her own safety. Truth is pictured as attacked, fallen, trampled underfoot, and unable to rise. The times are so evil that an upright man finds his life in danger. By now Manasseh was already king, and Isaiah must have realized his danger. In the face of such horrible conditions, God offers Himself as Savior and Intercessor. Judah is an example of the helplessness of the entire human race in its struggle against sin and the forces of evil. Without divine intervention mankind has no hope. Isaiah pictures Christ as an armed warrior entering into the struggle for man's salvation. He clothes Himself with righteousness and salvation, and, from the east and the west, other people will pour in like a flood because they revere His glory. There will always be people who are faithful to Him.

> *Justice is personified and pictured as having fled away for her own safety. Truth is pictured as attacked, fallen, trampled underfoot, and unable to rise.*

Chapter 60 reveals the future glory of Jerusalem. Darkness is a symbol of God's absence. Light is a symbol of His presence. The sun and moon will no longer be needed. God will be her everlasting light and glory. Her days of sorrow will have ended. The gates will be kept open because there will be nothing to fear. Nations and kings and the returning children of the Jews will come from afar, bringing their wealth and treasures. Jerusalem's people will be righteous and live there flourishing forever. Isaiah was the first and greatest Hebrew prophet to clearly see Israel's worldwide evangelistic responsibility. His clarity of vision and vivid presentation of Israel's world task of missions dominates many sections of his writing. This chapter is one of those.

Chapter 61 is one of the most striking chapters of the book. Jesus applied it to Himself in His hometown. The subject matter is closely related to that of chapter 60. Christ came "to proclaim liberty." The phrase itself and the thought it expresses are taken from the proclamation made in the year of jubilee. The time would come when all the sorrows of the past would be over, and God's people would bedeck themselves as for a gala occasion of festivity and joy. Former enemies would come and help them. All of God's people—not just the descendants of Aaron—would be priests in the great task of bringing the Gentiles to a knowledge of the true God. Everyone would recognize that God's people are especially blessed and favored by Heaven. Just as He makes gardens grow, God is the only one who can produce righteousness and praise in His people.

Chapter 62 continues the theme of chapter 61 without interruption. Christ is still speaking, describing the glorious future God has planned for Jerusalem and His people. All of the inhabitants of heaven have set aside their own comfort and other tasks in order to focus on earth's emergency. All obstructions were to be removed so everyone could come into the city. God is coming back with His reward and gifts. The Holy people will eternally enjoy life together with Him. The New Jerusalem will be the capital city and the residence of God.

Chapter 63 begins with the Messiah's solitary victory over all opposition. Nobody helped Him. Then there is a prayer of praise and thanksgiving when Zion remembers the lovingkindness and tender mercies of God that have been extended in spite of Israel's repeated transgressions. Christ intervened again and again on their behalf. Both the word for Savior and the name Jesus are derived from the same root word. It was Jesus Himself who suffered with them, carried them like a father, and protected them. Their unfaithfulness caused them to forfeit God's protection and caused Him to appear to be their enemy. Actually, the judgments that befell them had a merciful design. God was seeking the ultimate salvation of each individual. God's power became known everywhere in that part of the world when He rescued them from Egypt by sending Moses and parting the Red Sea so they could easily walk across. His glorious arm was poetically the means by which God had wrought such mighty acts for the deliverance of His people. Isaiah's prayer asks for God's help like He had given in the past.

In the Old Testament, God is represented as doing that which He does not prevent. Because people are free moral agents, God does not prevent them from following the way of evil if they so choose. But God permits trial only if it results in good. Babylon was coming to Jerusalem. The temple would be destroyed and their city torn down. They were fearful and discouraged. Isaiah's confession on behalf of the

An Outline of Isaiah

people here reaches its lowest depth of anguish. They feel themselves to be deeply humiliated in that God has seemingly rejected them, and they beg humbly that they may not be cast off utterly. It is that spirit of utter dejection and despair that causes them to lift up their eyes to Heaven in the prayer that opens the following chapter.

Chapter 64 begins with the verse that is the last verse of chapter 63 in the Hebrew text. Only our God acts on behalf of His people. God welcomes those who joyfully live harmoniously with Him. Not only do they keep God in their conscious memory; they also do that which a knowledge of God and divine instruction should lead men to do. Our natural human nature is totally depraved. Just as a leaf separated from a tree soon withers and dies, the same is true of a person separated from Christ. The wind carries a leaf farther and farther from the parent tree. Likewise, sin sweeps man farther and farther away from God and hurries him on toward death and destruction. So this prayer is a pathetic plea for mercy. God was still in a position to help. In light of the coming Babylonian captivity, (and maybe also in light of the desperate times they were living in during King Manasseh's reign), Isaiah pleads that God's punishment may not last too long and that it may not be too severe. He describes the captivity as if it had already taken place. Actually, the Babylonian captivity would not happen for another century, but his views of it had been vivid, and probably he did not know exactly when it would take place. He closes by asking God whether He would keep silent and continue to afflict His people.

Chapter 65: In response to the prayers of chapters 63 and 64, God gives a grand comparison of the life and fate of those who are on His side and those who choose not to be. Many Gentiles are seeking and finding Him. He had patiently called to the Israelites for many years while they rebelliously went their own way. God was endlessly wounded by the attitudes and actions of the Israelites who made a high profession of holiness but constantly worshiped idols. Renegade Jews at times were initiated into heathen mysteries which it was thought produced a superior type of holiness. This was smoke in God's nostrils. He detested it.

Not all of the people were wicked, and not all would be destroyed. Others who had not known about Him were becoming part of His family. Those of Judah who were righteous among them would be spared and restored to their beautiful land. His people would be greatly blessed.

In describing the joys of the new creation, Isaiah is referring to the time preceding the final eradication of sin and sinners, after the Messiah had come and died, but before the resurrection and immortality. According to the Old Testament prophecies, there would be some time when people would live long lives but finally die. Because those promises were provisional, things did not turn out that way. These promises will be fulfilled after the second coming. The picture of a new and better world gives strength and courage as we meet the trials of the present.

Chapter 66: God is not concerned with how large a residence we build for Him. He desires a humble, contrite, and obedient spirit in those who worship Him. In the severe treatment that came upon Judah, the Lord had a wise and merciful purpose. What He could not accomplish through them in their own land, He would accomplish by scattering them among their heathen neighbors. In the meantime, Isaiah and others who trembled at God's word would see the tables turned on those who hated and excluded them. "Let the Lord be glorified so that we can see your joy" was a taunt used against the righteous. Israel's failure to fulfill the divine purpose was not due to any deficiency of divine grace. The time would come when the righteous will rejoice. But judgment will come on the wicked who mingled heathen rites with the worship of Jehovah. The consecration and purification ceremonies were probably initiatory rites into heathen mysteries. The groves used for worship were frequently the scene of cruel and immoral religious ceremonies. God had told them to destroy these places, but instead they participated in the disgusting practices of worshiping abominable and revolting objects. They had sunk to the lowest depths of degradation.

The prophet's mind was projected forward to the time of the restoration after Babylon. The land was long desolate, but with the return of the exiles it would suddenly throb with new life. If the Jews in exile had heeded the message of the prophets, the restoration would have been as dramatic and as glorious as here described. The seriousness of God's purpose is emphasized. God would not permit the temporary failure of Israel to frustrate His plan for the ages. The spread of knowledge about God would result in people from all nations coming to Him at Jerusalem. Those who are on God's side will have eternal life. We can be just as confident of that as we are that the new heavens and the new earth will endure. All of us will joyfully worship together every week in eternal recognition of Christ as the Creator and as the Re-Creator.

Poetic language regarding the dead bodies of the wicked has to be thoughtfully interpreted. The bodies were dead, not living. The worms were still living because they hadn't finished eating. The translation could be "not died yet" and the fire "not yet been quenched." Just as forest fires naturally go out when they have consumed what is available, so it would be with this fire. At that time, the garbage from Jerusalem was thrown out in a valley where the fire would consume it, but because garbage continued to be thrown there day after day, it is probable that the fire continued burning.

This cannot be applied to eternity. The fire that consumes the wicked at the end of the millennium will go out when there is nothing left to burn.

> The destruction will be complete and the wicked will have suffered the sorrow of missing out on all the good things God had offered, as well as the disgrace of not having a burial. Afterwards, God will wipe the tears from all our eyes and from His own as well. Then we will have the infinite privilege of watching him restore and recreate the new heavens and the new earth. Don't let anything steal your chance of being there on that momentous day to witness such an incredible event in the company of all the saved, with your elder Brother Jesus, our Savior!

Additional Sources

Andrews Study Bible, New International Version. Berrien Springs, Michigan: Andrews University Press, 2019.

Gane, Roy. *Altar Call.* Newcastle upon Tyne, UK: Diadem Books, 1999.

Isbouts, Jean-Pierre. *The Biblical World: An Illustrated Atlas.* Washington, D.C.: National Geographic, 2007.

Nichol, Francis D, ed. *Seventh-day Adventist Bible Commentary.* Hagerstown, MD: Review and Herald Publishing Association, 1978.

Quimby, Paul E. *Messages of the Prophets.* Mountain View, California: Pacific Press Publishing Association, 1946.

Thiele, Edwin R. *The Mysterious Numbers of the Hebrew Kings.* Chicago, Illinois: The University of Chicago Press, 1951.

Whiston, William, trans. *Josephus: Complete Works.* Grand Rapids, Michigan: Kregel Publications, 1964.

TEACH Services, Inc.
P U B L I S H I N G

We invite you to view the complete
selection of titles we publish at:
www.TEACHServices.com

We encourage you to write us
with your thoughts about this,
or any other book we publish at:
info@TEACHServices.com

TEACH Services' titles may be purchased in
bulk quantities for educational, fund-raising,
business, or promotional use.
bulksales@TEACHServices.com

Finally, if you are interested in seeing
your own book in print, please contact us at:
publishing@TEACHServices.com
We are happy to review your manuscript at no charge.

www.ingramcontent.com/pod-product-compliance
Lightning Source LLC
Chambersburg PA
CBHW051110160426
43196CB00028B/2316